Surrey and the Motor

SURREY AND THE MOTOR

BY

Gordon Knowles

Published by the Surrey Industrial History Group

© Gordon Knowles, 2005

ISBN 0 9538122 3 5

The moral rights of the author have been asserted

The Surrey Industrial History Group is a Group of the Surrey Archaeological Society. It aims to study, record and where appropriate preserve the remains of the former industries of the county. It holds meetings, lectures, visits and social events and publishes a regular Newsletter. Further information may be obtained from the Membership Secretary, SIHG, c/o Surrey Archaeological Society, Castle Arch, Guildford, GU1 3SX and from the Group's website: http//www.surreyarchaeology.org.uk/sihg

Cover: An AC Rally at Brooklands

Printed by J W Arrowsmith Ltd., Bristol.

Contents

List of Illustrations

Foreword

The late Francis Haveron started gathering material for a book of this title in the early 1990s. He corresponded with a large number of people in the course of his research, including myself. I had also worked on researching the motoring history of the county, largely for my adult education lecture series, and Francis and I exchanged much information, adding to each other's knowledge.

I thought at the time that Francis had beaten me to it, for I had felt that there was the basis of a book in my research material. Ah well, I thought, good luck to him. Unfortunately Francis' health deteriorated in the mid 1990s and his researches and draft writings gradually slowed to a halt. Francis had several falls following an attack of double vision, he died following a serious fall on 19 August 2000. Francis Haveron had been one of the founders, and the first Secretary, of what became the Surrey Industrial History Group of the Surrey Archaeological Society and almost single-handed ran for some 20 years the very successful SIHG winter programme of lectures held at the University of Surrey in Guildford. He stood down from this task at his request in 1994 and also from the committee of SIHG in 1996 when he was made a Vice-President in recognition of his work for Industrial Archaeology in the county.

When Francis' papers were being gathered together after his death his widow Pam asked SIHG if we were willing to take the motoring research over and find someone who would continue the project. I willingly agreed, and although it has taken some time due to other commitments, here is my book, dedicated to the memory of Francis Haveron. I must emphasise that my writing style is different from that of Francis and although I have used some of his research material I have amplified it and incorporated much more of my own into this book. There would have been too many obvious "seams" if I had attempted to leave his original draft material unchanged and then added to it from my own researches which I brought to a close at the end of March 2004.

Gordon Knowles
Great Bookham
May 2004

1

CHAPTER 1

Why Surrey?

There is more to historic Surrey in an industrial and transport sense than a first glance would suggest. The county has had a relatively tranquil passage through the centuries of tribal strife, invasions, uprisings, riots, wars and assassinations. Equally the social and economic upheavals of the industrial revolution largely passed it by. We have no coal mines, shipbuilding or steel works and have had little heavy industry. The textile industry in mediaeval Guildford and Farnham did not survive and the Godalming frame-knitting hosiery industry was not on a very large scale. In the twentieth century we have of course seen the birth and death of aircraft manufacture in the county. But fortunately not so in vehicle manufacturing. We still have one major manufacturer of bus and fire engine chassis, and several small specialist car manufacturers. We have also seen the recent introduction of a specialist off-road vehicle manufacturer, so all is not lost.

In transport terms in the county, we have had the pioneering Wey Navigation to Guildford, subsequently extended to Godalming, and parts of the Basingstoke and Wey & Arun Canals. The chief pressure for canal and subsequently railway development through the county was to connect London with the navy at Portsmouth and with overseas trade at Southampton. Then came the great push into suburbia eating up much of the county bordering London. So much so that a large slice of the county along the Thames was absorbed into London in the nineteenth century, with more following in the twentieth. The railways developed to cater for that new breed of worker, the commuter.

So to the motor. We have had no major volume car or commercial vehicle manufacturer, but we have had over 100 different makes of car produced in the county at one time or another. Some of these progressed no further than a single prototype, others became small volume specialist manufacturers.

Some of the more important ones are given detailed coverage in the book, an A to Z appendix briefly describes the rest. Cars, buses, commercial vehicles, fire engines, dust carts and even lawn mowers and tanks all appear, although the latter two only in passing. It is the aim in this book to set out the relationship between the County and the motor vehicle over more than a century in which they have existed together. Sometimes the County has influenced the motor, sometimes the reverse.

Surrey's proximity to London accounts for much of the activity over the years. Kings occupied Guildford Castle and built their royal palaces at Richmond, Kew, Oatlands (Weybridge) and Nonsuch (Cheam). The aristocracy followed the crown, buying themselves handsome country estates. There followed a need to visit the estates frequently leading to the turnpike system which attempted to improve the quality of the roads. The milestones along the way were not only a useful guide to the traveller but also a means of demonstrating to him in whose territory he was. For example, the so-called 'White Lady' direction post at Esher erected for the Duke of Newcastle, is reputed to have been done for the benefit of visitors to the duke's home at Claremont as much as for the traveller. Another instance were the 'Pelham Buckles' still to be found on some milestones on the A22 indicating that the Pelham family not only owned the milestones but also the road and surrounding land.

White Lady direction post, Esher *Peter Tarplee collection*

The invention of the cycle is of interest to us as it was only a little in advance of the inventing of the motor car. It liberated middle-class Britain enabling many to venture out on their own from their town or village for the first time. They could travel without the need to keep, feed and stable a horse, or to own a carriage as the aristocracy did. Cycling clubs provided the friendship of like minds and as they ventured further away from home into the countryside, road surfaces slowly improved. The run from Kingston to Ripley down the Portsmouth Road was one of the first to gain popularity. The road had been turnpiked since 1749 but deteriorated and was virtually devoid of traffic after the railway had opened to Portsmouth. The cyclist needed as level a road as possible and a reasonable surface, both found on the road from Kingston to Ripley. To quote a local writer in 1881, "To no place in the whole island of Great Britain do more bicycles wend their way than to the quiet and pretty Surrey village of Ripley."

Often bicycles were made by the local blacksmith on a purely one-off basis, (e.g. Brox of Ottershaw), and many famous motor car firms are derived from successful bicycle manufacturers. The most well-known Surrey example is that of the Dennis brothers in Guildford, of which more later.

Another key factor in the improvement of the roads was a political one. David Lloyd George, who later on came to live at Churt in the south-west of the county, was Chancellor of the Exchequer in the early years of the twentieth century and in 1908 introduced a proposal in his budget to licence motor cars in order to raise money to be spent on the roads. We all know how far this ideal has moved in more recent times. It is a classic case of the Treasury taking money away with one hand and giving a little of it back, reluctantly, with the other. Licensing cars has been proved most useful to the police enabling the owners of vehicles to be traced and criminals located and prosecuted, unless of course the car in question has been stolen in the furtherance of crime. Unfortunately it is long gone since the Road Fund Tax was just that, it was the first of many laws passed, often regarded by motorists as petty, which have sometimes helped drive a wedge between the police and the motorist who sees himself as being an all too easy prey.

The ability to penetrate the countryside and roam almost at will was one of the factors in the rise in popularity of the motorcycle. The car had to stay on the road – at least until the arrival of the four-wheel drive off-road vehicle – whereas the motorcycle had the ability to go along the tracks and byways of the countryside. In doing so, it has incurred the wrath of landowner, walker, cyclist and horserider. The Act which enabled the motorcyclist to ride with impunity along some of the traditional countryside tracks, for instance the Ridgeway, has acerbated the bad feelings between them and horse riders and walkers.

During the late Victorian and Edwardian periods the rich engaged renowned architects to build them country houses, large and small. A house designed by Lutyens, with a garden by Gertrude Jekyll, was the epitome of taste and an indicator of wealth. Surrey has a number of these houses, the architect often having some difficulty in placing the 'car house' in a convenient place that was approved of by the owner. Although the car was another sign of wealth and status, it had to be hidden out of sight, often in a converted stable, or if in a new building in one that looked like one, so that the chauffeur could bring it out when his master called. The origin of the term 'chauffeur' is French, coming from 'chauffer' meaning 'to heat'. Your chauffeur initially was the man who stoked up your steam car or, more likely, heated up the petrol engine for you in readiness for a drive.

Roads and Motoring Legislation I – up to 1914

Until the Tudors finally destroyed the feudal system responsibility for the upkeep of public highways was one of the many duties laid upon landlords as one of the conditions of the tenure of their land. When the feudal system broke down this obligation fell upon the inhabitants of each parish. They were concerned only with the roads within the parish and consequently the main roads suffered. In the seventeenth century wheeled traffic significantly increased as industry and commerce developed, identifying the need for a better system. So in 1663 the first Turnpike Trusts were set up to levy tolls on travellers so that the roads outside parish boundaries could be maintained. By 1840 there were some 22,000 miles of turnpike roads in England, many of excellent construction, with over 8,000 toll bars.

Historically the state of the roads in Surrey had been strong north–south, crossing the Downs, but poor east–west, following the lines of the Downs. The Portsmouth Road had been of major importance as the most effective means of communication between the Admiralty in London and the Navy in Portsmouth, particularly in time of war when the English Channel was not a safe means of communication due to marauding French warships. The early nineteenth century telegraph system is a reminder of this, with the restored signal tower at Chatley Heath off the A3, close to Junction 10 of the M25, being a reminder of the importance of this route. The first toll road in the county was established in 1696 between Crawley and Reigate, though it was not fit for carriages until 1755. The Portsmouth Road, today the A3, was progressively turnpiked between 1711 and 1749; from Portsmouth to Petersfield in 1711, from Southwark to Kingston in 1718 and from Kingston to Petersfield in 1749. The Bath Road, today's A30 through Staines, was turnpiked in 1728 and the Brighton Road through Reigate progressively in 1718, 1755 and 1823.

The last turnpike road to be opened in Surrey was between Godalming to near Dunsfold in 1836. Pepys in his famous diary

Double Toll Gate at Merton *SIHG collection*

records that he often was obliged to travel down to Portsmouth from London on horseback to look after naval matters and that on one occasion he got lost in travelling from Cobham to Guildford, and after spending the night recuperating did the same the next day near Hindhead. Cobbett called Hindhead around 1800 "a god forsaken place" though said that the road from Guildford to Godalming was " the fairest in the kingdom."

Coaching inns, in towns where coaches stopped to change horses, provided food, drink and a bed if required. Some as well as providing a change of horses also had a heavy horse or two on hand to assist coaches up steep hills. The Wheatsheaf Inn is supposed to have kept such a horse to help up the Mount outside Guildford on the old turnpike road to Farnham.

George Gwilt was appointed County surveyor in 1782 at the age of 24, becoming responsible for the rebuilding and widening of the mediaeval bridges at Cobham, Godalming and Leatherhead. The county magistrates oversaw the parishes and local rates supported by tolls from travellers paid for road improvements, such as they were. The turnpiked roads were improved both in terms of line and gradient as well as the surface being maintained and improved. The fact that the toll-collecting system was abused, and tolls diverted into the collectors' pockets, did not assist in improving matters.

8

Tadworth Toll Gate 1870 *SIHG collection*

The 1835 Highways Act codified the turnpike trusts' and parishes' responsibilities, and rural, urban and county councils were eventually set up but without, initially, control over the highways. In the same year, 1853, 'Surrey in London', in the north-east of the county, became part of the responsibility of the Metropolitan Board of Works, established to co-ordinate public works in the metropolis. At first in 1862 parish councils and then later highway districts were given powers to raise funds and to maintain and improve the roads in their area. In 1888 Lord Salisbury's Tory Government, with all party support, passed the Local Government Act which brought about the demise of Surrey in London, by transferring the boroughs of Southwark, Lambeth and Wandsworth to the new London County Council. Surrey at a stroke lost some two-thirds of its area and population. At the same time Croydon was given County Borough status.

Under the act new county councils were created, taking control out of the hands of non-elected magistrates and into those of councillors elected by the resident ratepayers on a similar basis to that existing in the boroughs. County boundaries were altered, but none as severely as in Surrey. Control over main roads in the counties was handed over to the new county councils. The first Surrey County Council was elected on 15 January 1889 and Mr. C H Howell was appointed County Surveyor with responsibility for bridges and major roads. He was then aged 62 and had been surveyor to the magistrates since

1860. When he retired in 1893 he was succeeded by his son Frank. In 1895 the last Turnpike Trusts were wound up.

The early years of Surrey County Council saw no major problems on the main roads, for since the coming of the railways they were no longer the major through routes for passengers or commerce. The roads from London through Kingston and Guildford to Portsmouth and through Croydon to Brighton, which had once been busy with coaches and wagons, had for fifty years been superseded by the railways and the fastest regular traffic on them was the pleasure cyclist. The roads were surfaced with water-bound macadam; broken stone, which under the weight of the steamroller and traffic with solid wheels, bound together to form a solid surface. Pedestrians would be covered, depending on the time of year and the weather, in either dust or mud from the ridden horse or heavy farm cart in the country, and from horse-drawn delivery vans, cabs, omnibuses and private carriages, as well as by the new bicycles, in the towns. It was reported that "in populous and badly scavenged areas, the dust would consist largely of dried horse dung."

Steam traction was used for heavy haulage. In the west of the county in 1900, when the Boer War increased military activity, the Aldershot and Wrecclesham roads suffered from War Department traction engines, "which only stopped when the roads beyond the county boundary broke up altogether". Why

Hand tarring on the London road at Ewell 1905 *SIHG collection*

the authorities should use road haulage for these large loads from Aldershot to Shorncliffe in Kent instead of using the railways is unknown. In 1904 engines carrying materials for the building of the mansion at Polesden Lacy damaged the Dorking Road and Bridge Street and the town bridge in Leatherhead. A major problem was the steam-hauled 'wagon train', which could consist of a locomotive, coal tender, water barrel and up to ten wagons, more in the case of the "showmen in Kingston and military trains from Aldershot attempting to navigate through the centre of Guildford". They could neither negotiate the "narrow streets and sharp turnings in Kingston or Guildford nor the winding country roads". Under the 1898 Locomotive Act the County Council attempted to pass by-laws limiting wagon trains to three wagons, but the measure failed to gain Parliamentary approval.

Towards the end of the nineteenth century a new menace was spreading fear and causing expense – the motor car. In July 1895 John Henry Knight of Farnham deliberately flouted the law and was prosecuted for "using a locomotive without a licence and exceeding a speed of 2 mph", contrary to the requirements of the 1865 Locomotive Act. John Henry Knight, a pioneer of motoring, will appear again later on in our story. Knight helped set up the Self Propelled Traffic Association which succeeded in getting the infamous Red Flag Act abolished.

The turn of the century saw considerable antagonism towards the 'new-fangled' motor car, and in particular what was seen as the fast and dangerous way they were being driven. In 1899 Cobham parish council was complaining of 'excessive motor car speeds', and the next year the Chief Constable of Surrey, Captain Sant, issued "a caution to cyclists and the drivers of motor cars in respect of furious driving and riding on highways … should this be insufficient I shall be obliged to have recourse to more stringent measures". Captain Sant quickly found himself with a nationwide reputation as the man who hated motor cars and motorists and was seen to 'persecute' them unmercifully. Sant had served in the Northumberland Fusiliers and had been Chief Constable of that county before taking up his appointment in Surrey on the first of September 1899 at the age of 36, at a salary of £500 plus £150 allowances for accommodation. He was in office until 1930 whereafter there was a less aggressive, but still positive, approach by the county police towards the motorist.

In the years leading up to 1914 attempts to control the 'speeding motorist' were well in hand. In the county the A3 near

Ripley was a popular spot with the police. Captain Sant set up speed traps to catch the unwary, and his actions were directly responsible for the setting up of the Automobile Association. Each member displayed a membership badge prominently on the front of his car. The AA patrol would place himself strategically some way along the road before a police speed trap and would salute a member as a warning of what lay ahead. In 1905 an AA patrol was fined for "obstructing a police officer in the execution of his duty, by saluting members to warn of a speed trap". Subsequently, until recent times, patrols saluted in recognition.

The press cartoonists had a field day. Lawson Wood in the Sketch identified an officious policeman at the scene of an accident as 'The Surrey Policeman'. A Punch sequence, 'A Day on the Ripley Road', showed a driver's progress being halted by 'an affable detective with a stopwatch.' Another sequence by Frank Gillet in the Daily Graphic showed motorists at Ripley being warned to slow down and the policeman's discomfort at being denied an easy arrest.

Those who were caught were often acid in their comments in court. Lord Onslow, in 1902, proposed a critical motion at the Quarter Sessions. In 1905 a Guildford magistrate stated from the bench that "a crusade was being waged against the motorist", and in 1908 Sir Archibald Macdonald summoned two policemen for perjury following his conviction for furious driving.

In May 1903, "the General Purposes Committee of Dorking Urban Council recommended that the Council should write to the Dorking Brick Company asking them to be good enough to give instructions, if practicable, that the traction engine used by them for haulage purposes should not pass through the town at an earlier hour than 7 am and at the same time to point out that the rate of speed of such engines appeared to be greater than that provided for under the Highway and Locomotives Act. Councillor Tebbs thought it was a disgraceful nuisance to have the heavily laden traction engine passing through the town at a fast rate at five o'clock every morning and heartily endorsed the committee's recommendation". This seems to be a mild rebuke and was couched in less vociferous language than other complainants.

The County Surveyor reported in 1908 that "heavy goods traffic between Farnham and Guildford would not continue to use the Hog's Back road if the railway companies would lower their rates". He also noted that "a bus service was planned from

Cranleigh to Guildford to meet the fast London trains on the London and South Western lines as the London, Brighton and South Coast Company timed their branch line service through Cranleigh to Horsham to keep passengers off the rival service."

In 1909 the Government had set up The Roads Board to make grants from the revenue received from vehicle licensing and petrol taxation introduced by the Chancellor, David Lloyd George, in his budget of that year.

Surrey County Council was also in the forefront in experiments with new surfacing materials and in improving bends and gradients on the main roads. In 1901 both Guildford and Kingston bridges were widened and reconstructed. Tarring was initially found to churn up when wet and granite chippings were not as effective as flint. From 1909 there was an annual programme of tar spraying and gritting on many major roads leading into and out of towns. The County Council minutes record that "tradesmen's carriers and lorries broke up the road surface, often because they are overweight".

In 1911 tar-macadam, a mixture of tar or bitumen, and sand or slag, was being used on the Portsmouth Road as far as Godalming, it had been first used experimentally in 1905 on the stretch between Esher and Cobham. The surface eliminated dust and was relatively impervious to water, but as the hard top was generally less than one inch thick, the roads remained vulnerable to rutting and pot-holing from the action of the motor vehicles, virtually all of which were fitted with solid rubber tyres on

Tar making machine at work in Horley *SIHG collection*

Dorking tar machine *SIHG collection*

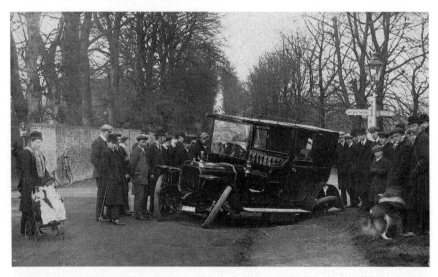

A minor accident draws the crowds in Reigate Road, Ewell 1911 *SIHG collection*

narrow profile wheels. The County Surveyor, Alfred Dryland, who had succeeded Frank Howell in 1908, proposed that the council should set up its own asphalt plant to save money. By 1914 this was built at Dorking and became the first county council owned and operated asphalt plant in the country.

Overloaded goods vehicles were common. as the County Council found out when they installed their first weigh-bridge on the Portsmouth Road, also in 1914.

The County Council minutes in 1909 record that the speed limit had been fixed at 10 mph and that the number of cars registered in the county in 1908 was 388, motor cycles was 239, manufacturers of motor vehicles 10, and licensed drivers numbered 5289. It was also recorded that it would take 2–3 years to change the surface on all main roads in the county from gravel to tar with granite chippings. The raw materials were some 62% of the cost of road maintenance. It was noted that the Portsmouth and Brighton roads had more traffic than any others out of London. Traffic on the Kingston to Putney road was now averaging 1,000 motor vehicles per day and it was also reported by the County Surveyor that, at Godstone, steam-traction haulage of sand was badly damaging the roads.

A survey was made in 1909 over seven days on the Malden to Coombe road and 6,136 motor car and motor cycle movements were reported, together with 400 motor vans, 95 steam wagons, 1,136 horse wagons, 544 horse vans, 715 carts, 527 4-wheeled carriages, 344 2-wheel carriages, 7,742 bicycles, 260 horses and 76 military horse vehicles. The bicycle was paramount, but 6,536 motor vehicles overshadowed 2,466 horse movements.

Kingston bridge was to be widened, and the surveyor reported that the new Car Tax Licence income was to be used for the Road Improvement Fund. Little did he know how it would soon be diverted for ever into the Treasury funds. In 1910 the Council minutes recorded that there was an increase of traffic on the Cobham to Old Woking road going to the new motor racetrack at Brooklands. There were continual references during the year to road surfacing improvements, and in particular that the Portsmouth Road, the busiest in Surrey, was now mostly tarred, and in fact that over half the main roads in the county were now tarred.

By 1912 motor traffic was equalling or surpassing horse-drawn traffic on all the busiest main roads, there were 700 cars and motor-cycles per day even in winter on the Portsmouth road at Thames Ditton, reducing to 300 at Ripley. Motor traffic between Epsom and Ewell was also running at 300 a day. On each of the Brighton roads, at the top of Reigate Hill and south of Redhill, it was 200 a day.

The 1913 annual report by the Surveyor noted that the tar macadam road east of Kingston had weathered well during its

15

A tank at Farnham level crosing causes traffic problems in the 1930s
Chris Shpheard collection

first winter, but that there had been some deterioration during the second year. Slag tar macadam seemed to be the best surface of the rest, Kent rag tar macadam was acceptable only under moderate traffic conditions. The A3 had been converted to a bituminous surface, there had been few complaints of slipperiness. It was much better for self-propelled vehicles and horses had got used to the sanded surface in wet weather. The need to find the best road surface was obviously taxing the Surveyor. One that was safe and did not rapidly deteriorate and yet was cost-effective was sought. Water-based macadam was discarded, a dense asphaltic composition was favoured. A survey showed that the County Council should set up its own direct labour organisation to make and lay road materials, it was claimed that they could cut the cost of contractors by some 25%.

London had used bitumen with sand for 30 years, concrete foundations proving unnecessary. It was agreed that Surrey would use bitumen at Kingston Vale, Godalming and Bagshot. £10,000 was voted for improvements to the Portsmouth Road, including widening at Ripley. The use of wood blocks at Epsom was sanctioned. The police were granted powers to demand to see a certificate of car registration. 827 cars had been registered in 1912, and 902 motor cycles, as had 28 manufacturers and 10,842 drivers. The considerable increase in income from

16

licensing had been partly offset by staff and salary increases. Where have we heard that before?

In 1914 Surrey was the first county to be taken in hand by the Road Board. A survey of dangerous corners was undertaken and heavy motor cars were prohibited from using the lanes around both Oxted and Godstone. There had been much damage from vehicles moving stone and sand from the quarries and lime pits. In 1914 the widening of Richmond bridge was sanctioned. There was a deputation regarding the heavy damage to Farnham Road in Guildford by motor vehicles. It was agreed to widen the road by the County Hospital. It was noted in the Council minutes that "there was a 132% increase in heavy motor cars registered in the county, and an increase of 201% in the County of London."

There were now, just before the outbreak of war in 1914, not only more and faster vehicles on the Surrey roads, but they were also getting progressively heavier, many more than the law permitted. Hence the setting up of a weigh-bridge on the Portsmouth Road, when it was found that one-third of the heavy motor cars weighed exceeded the registered axle weight and a sole traction engine weighed four tons four cwt. more than its licensed weight. "It is evident from the results so far obtained that overloading is very general, and it is most desirable that it be checked."

By the outbreak of war the surface of Surrey roads had been transformed, but the roads still mainly followed their old alignment, winding from village to village with many sharp bends. Two proposals were made for new roads; for Kingston on the Portsmouth Road, and for Sutton on the Brighton Road. The County Council undertook to consider these 'loop roads' – the 'by-passes' of the future – on their merits. A Government survey of 'curves and corners' was begun but the war intervened and any further road improvements were halted.

References
Surrey Through The Century; 1889–1989. Robinson, Surrey County Council 1989
Surrey History Centre – Surrey Constabulary records SRO CC98/3/2, 41SRO CC98/12/1
Surrey History Centre – minutes of County Council meetings
Dorking Advertiser May 1903

Roads and Legislation II – WWI and between the wars

On the outbreak of war in 1914 the Highways Department of Surrey County Council faced major problems. The War Office requisitioned two of the three lorries intended for the new asphalt plant and the general shortage of transport made it hard to obtain granite for road metal. Troop movements and the increased delivery of war materials by road was breaking up the surfaces. It was reported that "four miles of the Portsmouth Road were practically destroyed by traffic to the army camp at Witley." The War Office eventually agreed to contribute to the repair of a number of roads, including the one from Farncombe station to the camp and to the Portsmouth Road and Quarry Street in Guildford.

Council minutes in 1915 noted that the licence office was moved to larger premises, and that red rear light legislation was endorsed; previously the SCC had declined to make appropriate by-laws. In 1916 the need for uniformity of rear lights was raised. It was suggested that cattle drovers should have them, but where should they be fixed? Resurfacing of London Road, Kenley was delayed as wages at the nearby aeroplane works were high, and whilst it was felt that the same rate should be paid to roadmen, the money was not available!

A conference was called in London to plan for post-war road building, as the need would be great and was recognised as being so. The term 'by-pass' was introduced for the first time. Outer by-passes were proposed for Kingston Vale and Esher, whilst inner by-passes were planned for London Road in Kingston and at Thames Ditton. A by-pass for Sutton and a new bridge at Richmond were also contained in the proposals. Importantly it was felt by the conference that central government should pay the bulk of the cost.

Prior to WWI little attention had been paid to the nation's roads by central government. The Mercantile Marine Department of the Board of Trade looked after shipping and other branches of the BOT looked after railways, tramways, canals, harbours and docks. The little attention paid to roads was through the Road Board, but mostly matters were left to County or Borough Councils.

But in 1919 the Ministry of Transport was established by Act of Parliament to oversee all transport on land, by road and rail, by inland waterways and in the air, but excluding shipping which was left with the Board of Trade. During the next twenty years the responsibilities of the new department were continually being widened, particularly by the Road Traffic Act of 1930 and the Road and Rail Traffic Act of 1933. These had been set up following the reports in 1928, 1929 and 1931 of the Royal Commission on Transport. The first report was entitled *Control of traffic on roads* and the second *Licensing and regulation of public service vehicles*. These two resulted in the 1930 Act, which set up Licensing Authorities for public service motor vehicles. Once an operator obtained his licence, after rigorous investigation, he was protected against unlicensed competition. The outcome was a series of mergers between haulage companies bringing more stability to the industry. The Commission criticised the practice which had developed whereby the Treasury took a 'rake-off' before handing over monies to the Ministry of Transport. This practice continued until 1937 since when the Road Fund has derived its main revenues from monies directly allocated by Parliament.

The third report in 1931 on *Co-ordination and development of transport* resulted in the setting up under the 1933 Act, following the Salter Conference, of a system of 'A', 'A contract', 'B' and 'C' licences for goods vehicles. An 'A' licence was a public carrier's awarded for general haulage work for reward, an 'A contract' licence was awarded where goods of a specific company or individual alone would be carried for at least a year. A 'B' licence was awarded for carriage of the holders own goods and/or for restricted general haulage work as to a distance or commodity or both. A 'C' licence was awarded for the carriage of the holder's own goods only. This last category aroused considerable concern by companies who for example delivered a 15 ton load of their own goods from Newcastle to London, but were forbidden to seek out a return load, the lorry having to return empty. This was not economic, nor in the interests of saving fuel, although this was not really a consideration in the thirties.

In Surrey the nineteen-twenties were marked by rapid population growth and the spread of suburbia and by the electrification of commuter rail routes by the Southern Railway. These rail services were speedier and were supplemented by improved bus services and the new Northern underground line to Morden. London's overcrowding was being relieved, and the fields between the towns and villages of north-east Surrey were built over until by the end of the thirties the built-up area extended almost unbroken, except for parks and deliberately preserved open spaces, south to Caterham, south-west to Leatherhead and west to Woking.

The population of the county increased by more than 25% in ten years, from 739,402 in 1921 to 947,846 in 1931. This rate continued until the outbreak of war in 1939 when it had reached 1,250,000. Within the county the greatest increase was in the metropolitan fringe and in the line of towns between Caterham and Epsom the population more than doubled in numbers between the wars.

Vehicle registrations in 1913 had been 8,578, by the end of the war in 1918 these were down to 3,996. The year after in 1919 saw a rise again to 11,540, which continued ever upward thereafter. There was thenceforth a continued decline in the number of licences issued for horse-drawn vehicles. Motor Hackney carriages now outnumbered horse-drawn ones. In 1919 the AA were granted permission to erect their first 'sentry box' on the Hog's Back at the Wanborough and Puttenham crossroads.

The Ministry of Transport set up three Highway Divisions, concerned with Classified Roads, Trunk Roads and Traffic and Safety. Class I Classified roads were the important ones connecting large centres of population and other roads so classified because of the amount of traffic using them. The Road Fund contributed, and still does, 75% of the cost of construction, improvement and maintenance of these roads. Class II roads are ones forming important links between Class I roads and centres of population. These carry a 60% contribution by the Ministry.

Class III roads were introduced post WWII in 1945 and these are minor roads which carry more than local traffic and receive a 50% contribution from the Ministry. When the Ministry was set up it was realised that a national policy for highways could only be achieved if the Minister had direct control over the most important routes in the country. A Trunk road which passed through several different Highway Authorities suffered from the vagaries of their differing approaches to road surfacing, bridges, by-passes, widening etc. The result was often a patchwork of wide and narrow roads, well and poorly maintained, with good and indifferent surfaces. The Trunk Roads Act of 1936 gave the Minister direct responsibility for some 4,500 miles of the principal highways in the country. The total cost is met out of the Road Fund, the actual work being carried out normally by County Councils acting as agents. Post WWII, the Trunk Roads Act, 1946, amplified the powers of the Minister and a further 3,700 miles of important routes were designated as Trunk roads.

The Traffic and Safety Division of the Ministry of Transport was set up to work closely with local authorities over such matters as speed limits, via the Road Traffic Act of 1934, and more recent amendments. This Act laid down a limit of 30 mph in built-up areas, it can be applied outside these areas, and removed from them, by a parliamentary order. Matters such as waiting restrictions, parking, road signs, traffic signals and lighting all fall within this Division's responsibilities.

In London, the Minister was given wider powers through the London Traffic Act, 1924, and the London Passenger Transport Act of 1933. On the safety side driving tests are administered by the Division, being made compulsory for all new drivers in 1934. Driving Examiners are also Traffic Examiners and are responsible for enforcing licensing conditions granted for goods vehicles. The Division is also responsible for road safety propaganda, based on the precepts of the Highway Code.

In the county the Highway Department had by the nineteen-twenties identified that tar macadam was by far the superior surface for all roads. The problem was that the rise in traffic

Reigate tunnel, now pedestrianised *SIHG collection*

21

Building the Caterham by-pass *SIHG collection*

Building a bridge on the Guildford by-pass 1933 *SIHG collection*

numbers, and the increasing weight of the commercial vehicles using the roads, was causing more damage than could be rectified. Traffic was still being channelled into the centre of

Kingston and down Guildford High Street, through the centre of Epsom and Ewell and the narrow streets of Leatherhead and Dorking. Traffic was clogged and the towns were choked. By-passes were essential.

The first by-passes to be designated and started in the county, around Kingston on the Portsmouth Road, and Sutton on the Brighton Road, had been identified as long ago as the wartime conference and had in fact been first proposed before the 1914–18 war. They were both completed in 1927, although the shorter Betchworth and Bagshot by-passes, which had been started later, were completed in 1925.

Other by-passes followed in the thirties: Dorking, Ewell, Leatherhead, Mickleham and Banstead in mid-Surrey; Egham in the north-west; and Caterham in the east. The Caterham by-pass was the first dual carriageway by-pass in the county. In July 1934 the second major improvement on the Portsmouth Road, the Guildford and Godalming by-pass, was opened by the Minister of Transport. Much of this work was carried out as unemployment relief, receiving additional government grant in return for employing workers from the distressed areas in the north.

The schemes were not universally popular, some cases of what today we would refer to as nimbyism – not in my back-yard – appeared. 1,182 inhabitants of Ewell petitioned against the proposed Ewell by-pass in 1929 and Shere Parish Council protested against their proposed by-pass, which in fact was not built until after the 1939–45 war. In 1934 a by-pass south of Farnham was planned against the wishes of the District Council, which preferred a line to the north of the town, cutting through Farnham Park. From time to time the County Council found itself in opposition to the Ministry of Transport. When the Ministry proposed its A23 Merstham, Redhill and Horley by-pass, the County Council argued that the cross country A25 was more important: roads with "real commercial or military significance" should take preference over a route used mainly for pleasure motoring.

The new roads were not to be bleak thoroughfares. Trees and shrubs were planted. For example £1,252 was spent on planting on the Kingston by-pass, with the aid of grants from the Ministry of Transport and the Roads Beautifying Association. Elsewhere local amenity societies took the initiative. Leith Hill District Preservation Society, for instance, undertook planting on the new line of the A25 between Dorking and Brockham. In 1934 a 'horticultural foreman' was appointed in the County Engineer's

Department, and in 1938, with planting schemes completed or contemplated on forty miles of by-passes, he was given two assistants.

The Mickleham by-pass, cutting through a part of the Mole Valley, has been described as "one of the best pieces of twentieth-century road landscaping in the country". Unfortunately in the twenty-first century the dual carriageway from the roundabout at the Leatherhead end towards Dorking has been reduced again to a single lane following a number of accidents on the Mickleham bends. Strangely however the opposite carriage remains dualled in spite of a very dangerous right-hand bend almost opposite the B2209, the Old London Road, the scene of a number of cars failing to take the bend and carrying on into the undergrowth. Some say that it is not the bend as such which catches out the unwary, but rather the camber!

In the thirties existing bridges were widened and new roads built. Three major bridges were constructed to carry roads over the Thames. Those at Chiswick and Twickenham were both designed by the Middlesex County Engineer, Alfred Dryland, who had moved across from Surrey in 1920. Hampton Court bridge was built by the Surrey County Surveyor, W P Robinson, with Sir Edwin Lutyens as architect. The Victorian iron bridge which had served since 1865 was described in 1923 as "unfit for the heavy and fast traffic of the present day". A 10 mph speed limit was imposed until the new bridge could be built. It was sanctioned later in the same year as was a new road to meet it from the western end of the Kingston by-pass at the Scilly Isles roundabout. The bridge was opened in 1933, a year after the new road, Hampton Court Way.

Hampton Court bridge as designed by Lutyens included four classical brick kiosks at the corners. These were deferred at the request of the Ministry of Transport as an economy measure in 1932 and by the time the Ministry was willing to authorise the expenditure on them the County Council had decided that the bridge looked better without them.

With the growth of the county came a change in attitude as to the purpose of the new roads. In the nineteen-twenties the Kingston by-pass was welcomed as encouraging development and recouping some of its cost by the increase in rateable value of the area it served. By the end of the decade, building developments along the line of the by-pass were seen to be a hindrance and danger to the traffic and a threat to the Surrey countryside. Unfortunately 'ribbon development' was a feature

24

Wapses Lodge roundabout, Caterham *SIHG collection*

of by-passes everywhere, not only in Surrey. In 1930 it was decided that there should be no increase in the number of junctions on the by-pass and that housing scheme layouts should be submitted in advance of construction to the London Traffic Advisory Council. Future developments were built with subsidiary roads parallel to the main road. The by-pass soon became inadequate to serve the increase in traffic. Each new idea for controlling or easing the flow of traffic and for helping pedestrians was used: lights, roundabouts, pedestrian crossings and pedestrian-controlled lights.

In 1928 a London to Brighton Toll Motor Road was proposed. It would have been taken off the Kingston by-pass at Surbiton, across Epsom Common, under the Epsom to Chessington Road and the Epsom to Leatherhead Road. The route would then have been by tunnel under Pebble Hill by Betchworth lime works, across the Dorking to Reigate Road east of Buckland to Leigh and Newdigate and on to the county boundary near Rusper, Horsham.

There was considerable opposition to the proposals and the County Council convened a conference on 18 January 1929 which was attended by 50 representatives of the objecting bodies. Concern was expressed at the possibility of private parties gaining government approval to build the road and collect tolls. Such permission had hitherto only been granted to railway companies. There is nothing new in the present concept, in the form of the new M6 deviation around Birmingham, one would think that the idea had not been thought of before the twenty-first century.

There was concern over the building of a "speedway from London to Brighton", and also that the County Council might have to step in in the event of financial failings by the speculators. Although a Parliamentary Bill was proposed it was not proceeded with.

By 1936, it was recognised that any future road developments on the county would need to be dual carriageways. To cope with the traffic build up at the western end of the Kingston by-pass, an Esher by-pass was proposed, but was delayed first by the outbreak of war in 1939, and afterwards by post-war economic stringencies. One development which was proceeded with in the thirties was the demolition of the old Burford bridge on the A24 and the building of its modern successor, coupled with the construction of a dual carriageway in the form of the Mickleham by-pass.

The by-passes and new roads contributed to road safety by removing traffic from urban roads. By the mid thirties road accidents had reached alarming levels: of eighty four fatalities in 1936, 82% were pedestrians, motor cyclists or pedal cyclists. Most of the pedestrians killed were over forty: County Council minutes record that "they found it difficult to adjust to the abnormal increase in the volume and speed of the present day vehicular traffic". Used to sharing the roads, they would not give way to cars, "the deciding factors, at the last moment, are the youth and agility of the pedestrian". A joint study by the County Engineer and the Chief Constable showed that the Egham by-pass immediately halved the number of accidents as compared with the stretch of road through the town which it replaced.

There was still concern over 'excessive speeds' and Surrey was as notorious during the thirties, as it had been in the twenties, for what was seen by some as 'excessive zeal on the part of the police', and by others as 'reasonable attempts to reduce accidents and make life as pleasant for the non-motorist as seemed possible in the new age of the car.' The "Cobham mile" on the A3 was a notorious spot where speed traps were set up, others were on the Brighton Road for example, but in general they were anywhere on the new by-passes where speed was easy to achieve – and measure. The police in the county was not one body at this time. Guildford, Godalming and Reigate each its own borough police force, and largely went their own way.

The Reigate Superintendent, Col. Bleacher, was in many respects more forward looking than the others and set up a high-speed car section under the direction of Sir Malcolm Campbell, who held the rank of Inspector in the Special Constabulary. The cars included powerful Alfa-Romeos, among the fastest cars on the market at the time. In 1935 Bleacher also introduced a volunteer Special Constabulary Air Patrol with de Havilland biplanes – another first. Unfortunately when the borough forces were in due course amalgamated into the county force this air patrol was disbanded. There was not seen to be any use for it by the powers in charge at the time.

Meanwhile in the county force, PC John Baker became the first motorcycle patrol officer, the forerunner of many more over the years. In many parts of the county other measures to protect the pedestrian were put in hand. Footpaths were widened and new ones provided to separate wheeled traffic from pedestrians. The Education Department promoted road safety in schools and children's safety committees were set up throughout the county and school crossing patrols were provided. Child deaths and injuries were at once significantly reduced; the elderly took longer to adjust.

Although the best road surface had been identified well before the 1914–18 war, the scale of post-war building and resurfacing dwarfed all previous experience. The County Council, to ensure their sources of aggregate for roads, had in 1921 purchased a quarter of a million tons of slag from a disused iron works in Glaisdale, an iron mining village in the Cleveland Hills, together with a lease of the land on which it lay. They had opened their first asphalt plant in 1914 at Dorking, in 1921 a further plant was opened at Barnes, and an asphalt and tar macadam plant at Ewell. In 1939 a modern tarmacadam and asphalt plant was installed at the Council's depot at Merrow, outside Guildford.

By 1939 the main roads in Surrey had all been transformed and even on the minor roads the water-bound macadam, dusty in summer and muddy in winter, had been replaced by tarmacadam. It was just as well, for the increase in traffic was massive. In 1938 there were 127,193 motor vehicles licensed in the county compared with only 11,590 in 1919. The A3, A23 and A30 main roads were each taking 25,000 tons or more a day, ten times the level in 1914. In 1937 the Ministry of Transport took over responsibility for the maintenance of main roads, but they continued to employ the County Council for most of the work on them.

Meanwhile the Bressey-Lutyens report on roads in Greater London identified the need for a North and South Orbital Road, which was eventually to become the M25. The Surrey section was to run from Egham to Limpsfield. A new road from Victoria to Brighton, incorporating a stretch from Coulsdon to Crawley, was to become in due course the line of the M23, and an extension of the Chertsey arterial road from there to Camberley and into Hampshire foreshadowed the M3. The lines of development of the main Surrey arteries into the 1980s were laid down during these last years in the thirties.

There had been a lot of unofficial development in the county in the late twenties which persuaded the County Council to seek and obtain town planning powers through a Surrey County Council Bill in 1931. Two other causes, other than building development, threatened to blight the Surrey landscape at this time. One was the willingness of people to "settle down in broken-down vans, railway wagons, tramcars and other objectionable vehicles". Box Hill and the Upper Thames were particularly affected.

The other related threat to the countryside was when speculators sold plots of land for self-builders without making up roads or providing sewers and other essential services. This particularly affected mid-Surrey from Cheam through Epsom and Leatherhead to the Bookhams. The Clerk of Epsom Rural District Council observed that "parts of the rural district which a few years ago were places of great natural beauty are now hideous and to be avoided". Epsom and Guildford Rural District Councils took the lead in promoting Local Acts of Parliament to control this kind of unwanted and unfortunate development.

The County Council, in preparing for its own 1931 Bill, used aerial and ground level photographs of shanty development, 'roads' which were no more than deeply rutted mud, and a petrol station built out of packing cases. The 1931 Act gave the County Council powers to prevent these kinds of unwanted shanty developments. It also gave it powers to control petrol stations and the rash of advertising billboards which were disfiguring the countryside.

Petrol stations had been opening up to serve the new motorists on the new roads. Many of them were makeshift, garish and smothered in advertisements. In the next few years they were brought into line. The County Council passed by-laws: no filling station might be established in certain sensitive areas and in other rural areas the apparatus must be painted in a uniform colour, normally dark green. Advertisements at the stations were to be removed, the size and style of lettering was regulated and a standard sign, a vertical winged arrow, must be used. More generally in rural areas, advertisements were restricted and could be forbidden altogether.

The Surrey County Council Act of 1931 served as a precedent for other local Acts and its success encouraged the government to promote its own Town and Country Planning Act in 1932, and Restrictions of Ribbon Development Act, in 1935. In the same way Surrey's acquisition of land was the inspiration for the London County Council's green belt scheme and was to be the basis of the Green Belt (London and Home Counties) Act, 1938. Surrey led the way, influencing not only development within the county but also within London and eventually country wide.

As early as 1904 the London County Council had met the greater part of the cost of acquiring Marble Hill in Twickenham. Now in the nineteen thirties it began a major programme of acquiring, or helping other authorities to acquire, properties to form a 'Green Belt' around London. Between 1935 and 1938 seventeen properties were acquired for £500,000, of which Surrey County Council paid £170,000, London County Council £150,000 and the district councils within the county £125,000. Local landowners also contributed to these schemes which preserved their own views.

References
Surrey Through The Century; 1889–1989. Robinson, Surrey County Council 1989
Surrey History Centre – SRO 2200/1/2/2, 6: SRO CC 133: SRO CC 134: SRO 2183/3: SRO 2185: SRO 2181: SRO CC 2

Roads and Legislation III – post 1945

Motorways and Public Transport

Road use in the county by the public was restricted during the second world war, from 1939 to 1945, as it had been during the first. As between 1914 and 1918 military traffic was considerable and built up in large numbers in preparation for the invasion of France in 1944. The Canadian forces, who were based in Surrey in large numbers, amongst other roads built Young Street during the war, the south-western section of the Leatherhead by-pass. It was named after the Canadian engineer officer in charge of the work.

After the war the new roads proposed in the nineteen thirties began to take shape. The Abercrombie report gave high priority to the proposed North and South Orbital Roads and in 1947 the line of the South Orbital Road through Surrey was approved. In 1946 the Ministry of Transport asked the County Council to plan a new trunk motor road to supersede the A30 between Egham and the county boundary at Frimley. In 1952 a new motor road to supersede the A23 through the county was surveyed. The M25, M3 and M23 were all now well on the map, but no actual work had yet begun. The first post-war decade was one of cutbacks in expenditure on road improvements and maintenance.

Authorised expenditure and government grants in 1953–1955 were hardly greater than in 1937–1939, whereas the cost of work had trebled. In practice most of the work undertaken in the early post-war years was improvement of existing roads, notably the dualling of the Kingston and Guildford by-passes on the A3. As late as 1962 the County Council was expressing deep concern at the inadequacy of the Ministry of Transport's grants and was pressing for construction of the new motor and trunk roads to be expedited.

Traffic density was increasing fast. In 1946–1947 113,000 vehicle licences were issued in the county: by 1962–1963 the number was over 410,000 and was increasing by 10% each year. Traffic over Hampton Court bridge increased by 26.5% in the

M25 near junction 8 at Reigate *Chris Shepheard collection*

M23/M25 interchange at Merstham *Chris Shepheard collection*

two years 1960–1962. Fortunately, in the nineteen sixties the Government began at last to make finance available for the new roads. Construction began on the M3 and the first stretch, from the Hampshire border to Lightwater, was opened in 1971. In 1972 work began on the M25. The first sections in Surrey, from Reigate to Godstone and from Egham to Thorpe, were opened in 1976 and the motorway through the county was completed in 1985. Other main roads, including the A24 south of Dorking, the A31 between Guildford and Farnham, the A30 in Ashford and the A308 in Sunbury, were all dualled.

The Esher by-pass, planned well before the war, was finally opened in 1976. The County Council had since 1937 acted as agents for the 51 miles of trunk roads in the county. In the 1960s they became agents for motorway construction and thereafter partners with central government in the Road Construction Units, the headquarters of the South Eastern Road Construction Unit being based in Dorking, with a sub-unit at Guildford.

Parking was becoming a major problem. Fixed penalties and traffic wardens came to Guildford in 1963 and were extended to Farnham and Walton-on-Thames in 1966, to most other towns and villages like Oxshott and Cranleigh in 1967, and to the rest of the county in 1968. By 1972 the County Council decided that 'traffic management' was needed as "increasing traffic volumes outpace the construction of major improvement schemes". Parking controls were combined with increased provision of off-street parking. The pedestrian was again, as in the thirties, a victim of the growth in traffic volume and speed. Roads, it was stated, needed to be designed 'to keep the pedestrian alive'. Injury causing accidents in the Surrey Police Area were collated by computer and black spot junctions improved. The redevelopment of town centres, notably Redhill, Leatherhead and Epsom, gave scope for road improvements, linked there and elsewhere to restrictions on town centre usage by the motorist and the provision of car parks.

The redevelopment of the centre of Leatherhead continues into the twenty-first century. One scheme after another to 'improve' the pedestrianisation of the High Street has been started and then abandoned. Pleas to open it up once again to traffic to entice potential shoppers fall on deaf ears. Meanwhile the traffic goes around the gyratory system, strangers hardly aware of the existence of the High Street.

By the 1960s the growth of cars had badly hit public transport. The Beeching axe was swung on the Surrey railways, though much less fiercely than elsewhere. The County Council, concerned at the effect on residents and the roads, opposed the rail closures, unsuccessfully in the case of the Horsham & Guildford Direct line, but successfully in respect of the lines out of Oxted into Kent and the intermediate stations on the Reading to Reigate and Tonbridge line. The Council also protested, with

Ockley Green postbus 1973 *SIHG collection*

mixed success, at repeated increases in both bus and train fares.

The 1972 Local Government Act made the County Council the highway authority for all roads in Surrey, other than motorways and trunk roads. The Act also gave the Council new powers in the planning of transport policy. Bus services were now suffering from the decline generally in the use of public transport which had previously only seriously affected the railways. The County Council had already set up a Transportation Team and was making grants to support unremunerative, but identified as essential, bus routes.

The Ockley post bus was established, following the pattern often found in rural parts of European countries. In 1975 a Transportation Planning Unit was formed. It was able to co-ordinate road building and transport provision, even though the Council did not directly operate public transport, as was done elsewhere in the country. Bus routes were subsidised and a concessionary fares scheme introduced. By 1981 there were new developments such as the 'Rambler's bus' and the 'Downs link.' The need for County Council involvement was greatly increased with bus service deregulation in 1986. Operators were now free to run such services as they considered profitable and the Council subsidised the provision of socially necessary services and also produced comprehensive timetables covering the services of the competing companies.

As the county saw the completion of 100 years of motoring it faced the same problems on the roads which have confronted both the public and the elected authorities ever since the coming of the internal combustion engine. Traffic flows on A roads in Surrey are twice the national average and car ownership continues to rise relentlessly. Road improvements, as in the '930s, are being undertaken to remove traffic from towns and villages, to improve safety and reduce delays to traffic. Some successes have already been achieved in the new century, in particular a reduction in personal accidents, but the restraints of geography, Surrey's mixture of densely populated urban areas and protected landscapes, together with what seem permanent financial restrictions, limit the scope for further improvement.

A new phenomenon in the twenty-first century is the rapid growth of traffic calming measures and spy cameras. Road tables, humps, squares, diamonds, chicanes and pinch points all occur on some road or other in the county. Often they all seem to appear within the same small urban area. 'Kill that speed' is the cry, now supported by big brother cameras and speed restrictions on even open stretches of road. Some are cleverly sited to catch the unwary driver. 50 mph suddenly becomes 40 or even 30 mph on a straight falling gradient, to catch the unwary. Often such signs seem to bear little relationship to the volume of traffic, or population density at the particular spot. Captain Sant would approve I am certain. Once again there is an air of general distrust of the police among motorists. With pressure to obtain convictions, how much easier it is to catch the motorist who often unwittingly marginally exceeds the speed limit, or who overstays his ever increasingly costly parking, or commits some other minor misdemeanour, rather than the burglar who breaks into your home or the thief who breaks into your car to steal your radio. Oh yes, Captain Sant would enjoy it all I am sure.

In the new century the work of relating road improvements, patterns of private transport movements and the provision and cost of public transport to provide optimum mobility at least cost, has become an increasingly complex exercise involving sophisticated computer systems. The technical skill of building roads and bridges to withstand the ever increasing weight of traffic, exacerbated by the adoption of European standards for additional axle loads on heavy lorries, although still central to the work of the road engineers, is now complemented by modern techniques for predicting and shaping the transport needs in the forthcoming years in the county.

There have been two natural disasters in recent times which

both disorganised the road system in the county and put enormous pressure on local and county authorities to bring back order as quickly as possible. The first of these was in September 1968 when, following continuous heavy rain throughout the county, severe flooding took place. 5.81 inches of rain fell at Caterham and 6.21 at Painshill. Rivers overflowed in the south of the county on Sunday 15th September. Redhill, Gatwick, Dorking, Farnham, Guildford and Godalming were all affected. By evening mid-Surrey was suffering, notably Leatherhead. By Monday night the floods had reached Woking, the Moleseys, the Dittons, Walton and Weybridge, and large parts of these densely-populated and low-lying areas, receiving through the rivers Wey and Mole the greater part of the county's floodwater, were under water. The County Council worked with the army and health services to alleviate distress. The army erected Bailey bridges where existing bridges had been swept away and set up warning signs.

On 16th October 1987 the great hurricane swept across southern England, blocking roads with fallen trees and devastating whole tracts of countryside. The main roads were first cleared by emergency council crews, joined by private contractors. Over a thousand men were soon at work and after the following weekend only a few minor roads were still not cleared.

Much has changed on the roads in Surrey in the course of just over a century. The Portsmouth Road, which carried only horse-drawn traffic, bicycles and a few steam locomotives in 1890, carried 2,000 motor vehicles daily near Esher a quarter of a century later and 15,000 a day after half a century. One hundred years on, the Esher by-pass takes well over 50,000 a day, with a further number in excess of 30,000 still using the old route through the town centre. The modern A3 is fundamentally different from its predecessor in alignment, as the Kingston, Esher, Ripley and Guildford by-passes run almost into each other. More recently the road beyond Guildford has at last been duelled, and until the bottleneck at Hindhead is reached it is almost to motorway standard, except for the numerous side roads entering and exiting onto it, and the lack of any restriction on types of users. Hopefully the long-awaited tunnel will soon become a reality, improving both the journey for the motorist and the environment for the local and more general population.

References

Surrey Through The Century; 1889–1989. Robinson, Surrey County Council 1989

CHAPTER 5

The Pioneers

John Henry Knight

The genesis of the motor vehicle in Surrey was in the hands of John Henry Knight of Farnham, born in 1847 into a wealthy land-owning family who lived at Weybourne House. John Henry's father, a successful banker, also owned Vernon House in Farnham, now the town library, and a brewery as well as several farms. Young John Henry was taken to the Great Exhibition in 1851, he was only four years old, but even at that early age it inspired him as he grew up to turn to engineering and away from the family banking tradition.

He was fascinated by the railway and the mechanical revolution that was taking place slowly on the farm. He became an apprentice with Humphrey & Tenant, shipbuilders in Deptford, and on returning home in 1868 the twenty-one year old set about building a steam carriage. He aimed to improve on earlier attempts, such as the steam road carriage by William Hancock who, in 1834, had run a steam coach, the 'ERA' with fourteen passengers, from Paddington to Regents Park and the City for 6d a journey. Or Sir Goldsworthy Gurney whose coach was reputed to have touched 15 mph in 1827 on a return run from London to Bath, or Mr. Church who carried 40 passengers in his Omnibus, built for the planned 'London & Birmingham Steam Carriage Co.'

Thomas Rickett and the Americans, Walter Dudgeon and Sylvester Roper, had all built smaller vehicles designed to carry four or five passengers and be privately owned. Rickett sold three of his carriages in Britain but they were effectively driven off the road by the infamous Locomotive Act of 1865 which called for each locomotive to be limited to a speed of 4 mph in the country and a mere 2 mph in the town and proceeded sixty yards ahead by a man carrying a red flag. This enforced a walking pace of no more than four miles an hour, and was intended to warn horse-riders and horse-drawn traffic of a 'self-propelled machine.' The Act was brought in with steam traction engines in mind, but now included the smaller passenger-carrying vehicles as well. The legislation so restricted British engineers that their work was frustrated and any early advantage was passed to France and Germany where no such restrictive legislation was found.

Knight's steam car, never built for sale but merely to satisfy his engineering curiosity, had in its original form, one double action cylinder of 5 inch bore and 7 inch stroke driving 5 foot diameter rear wheels. The front wheels were smaller and were connected via a short axle to a steering tiller. Lacking a differential gear, it crashed on its first outing into a roadside bank, but recovered and was driven for a further 500 yards before two spokes in a wheel failed. Over the next few years various improvements were made, and some excellent runs were had, but also there were many mishaps. All Knight's runs were made against the existing law. Knight wanted to move on and sold the car in 1877, after it "had given much pleasure and several disappointments".

Knight had also turned his mind to inventing agricultural machines. In 1873 the 'Patent Digging Machine' was designed to dig over the hop fields of Badshot Farm which had till then been entirely dug by hand. It was built for him by Hetherington & Parker at Wey Iron Works at Alton and was driven by a continuous rope which ran round the field over a series of pulleys. The rope, powered by a single static steam engine, turned a horizontal pulley which was geared to the driving wheels of the digger. Cranks operated three forks at the rear which simulated the action of a man digging. The machine was steered by a man in front with a tiller digging the soil to a depth of 10 inches, but it kept breaking down, as did a second machine, also built at Alton. Two modified all-metal improved versions were built by Howards of Bedford and were more successful They worked continuously for five years, with a crew of two and two boys they could dig some three acres in a day.

The telephone had been invented in 1878 and a year later Knight installed one between Weybourne and Badshot Farm, it was one of the first in the country. By 1902 Knight had invented a brick-laying machine, a car speedometer, and a patent wooden tyre made of ash slats (because he was appalled at the price of rubber tyres). During WWI he invented a grenade-throwing catapult, which was seriously considered by the War Office as a trench weapon. He was a keen photographer and a collection of his glass slides is in Farnham museum, he also dabbled in the new science of colour photography. Knight wrote several books, including "Light Cars and Voiturettes" in 1902.

In 1884 Knight had married and moved to a new house,

Barfield, in the village of Runfold, just outside Farnham. It was here that in 1889 he developed his most successful invention, an oil engine, the patent jointly held with J E Weymann. The 'Trusty', running on paraffin, was one of the first British stationary engines. It was initially built for Knight by George Elliot in his Reliance workshop in West Street, Farnham. Later manufacture was undertaken by Clayton & Shuttleworth when over a 12 year period some 800 were sold. Visiting Paris in 1893, Knight saw Serpollet's steam car which made 15 mph, and he commented wryly that in Britain it would be restricted by law to 4 mph. Serpollet told Knight: "You English are a very clever people but your laws are bad, very bad."

Daimler and Benz

Knight was well aware that the world's motor industry had started in South Western Germany following the work of two men working independently at either end of the Neckar Valley in the late eighteen seventies and early eighteen eighties. They were Gottlieb Daimler and Karl Benz. Both men based their experiments on the principles established by Otto and Langen, following Otto's patent of the four-stroke concept in 1884. Daimler and Wilhelm Maybach built their first internal combustion engine powered vehicle in 1886, fitted with an air-cooled vertical single-cylinder engine of 1.5 hp with hot-tube ignition fitted into an ordinary horse-drawn carriage.

Meanwhile Karl Benz had in 1885 succeeded in designing and building the world's first workable car driven by an internal combustion engine. It was an organic unit of chassis and engine, unlike the Daimler which was a motorised horse carriage, hence the origin of the phrase, a 'horse-less carriage'. The Benz was a tricycle with the drive to the two rear wheels. The engine was an horizontal single-cylinder with a vertical crankshaft and a horizontal flywheel. It developed three quarters of a horse power and a speed of 8 mph was recorded on its first trial run. It had features still in extensive use today; a water-cooled engine, electric ignition, mechanically-operated inlet valve, and a differential gear.

Returning home from Paris, Knight mused over the outdated law in Britain which had prevented him getting very far with his steam carriage back in 1868, and was still in force. All self-propelled vehicles in England were governed by local regulations. They had to be licensed by the County Council and could only work during limited permitted hours in the day.

Worst of all was the maximum permitted speed of 4 mph in the country and 2 mph in town. There was later confusion over the 1878 amendment to the Act, and doubt as to whether a man carrying a red flag in front was still required.

In February 1895 Knight turned his attention to designing a light-weight motor tricycle powered by a single cylinder gas engine, a smaller version of the Trusty engine, adapted to run on Benzolene. The vehicle and engine was made for him by the Reliance engineering firm of West Street, Farnham, with George Parfitt, the foreman, in charge of the operation. (Parfitt had earlier worked at the Wey Iron Works where Knight's digging machine was first built).

The engine of the tricycle was placed in a longitudinal position at the rear of a wooden frame. There was a two speed transmission, initially by rope, whereby the drive, on different sized pulleys, was taken to a countershaft mounted across the middle of the chassis with power conveyed to the nearside wheel by chain. The single front wheel was steered by a tiller while the final drive was by chain to one of the rear wheels. Braking was by a contracting band on the rear axle, although a spoon brake on the solid rubber offside tyre was added later, plus a sprag or spike which could be let down to dig into the road if the car started to run back on a hill. The vehicle was a crude interpretation of the Benz car which Knight had seen and much admired.

Knight was on holiday in Switzerland in July 1895, when Parfitt completed the car and ran it on local roads early in the mornings to avoid the police. He wrote to Knight that " I went up to Passmoor bridge with two of us on her, and changed water there ... I certainly had the engine running some time before I set out there. This was in slow speed as I could not get enough slip on to start the engine with both ropes on; so I took off the fast speed rope ... went sailing along alright about 4 mph". When Knight returned he tried running the car on paraffin but soon reverted to benzolene, and eventually moved on to using gasoline. He also made a carburettor with a water jacket to keep it warm, replacing the hot tube ignition with an electrical system, making his own sparking plug from ¾″ diameter stoneware for insulators.

Salomons and Simms

Knight made another trip to Paris where he was technically unimpressed by a Panhard & Levassor car, but he wrote to the Times, "Why are none of these ingenious vehicles in use in

England? The reply must be that until the laws relating to Road Locomotion are in a more satisfactory state, few persons would venture to commence building motor carriages … Meanwhile we are losing a trade which in a few years might be of considerable value". Now was the time, he thought, to make a direct attack on the law. It is possible that Knight drew up his plan in conjunction with his friend Sir David Salomons, the Mayor of Tunbridge Wells, who had arranged an exhibition of imported cars at his home in early October 1895. Salomons own Daimler-engined Peugeot and a Panhard & Levassor, imported by Charles Simms and the Hon. Evelyn Ellis, were joined by two other cars which were demonstrated before a large crowd. Simms and Ellis had earlier illegally driven their car from the coast to Ellis's home in Windsor, and Ellis had driven with impunity around the town there. Perhaps the fact that he was related to Lord Howard may have had some bearing on the fact that the police ignored him. At this time there were probably no more than ten or twelve motor cars in England, none of which could legally be driven on a public road at more than 4 mph.

Simms and Salomons had earlier that year in 1895 set up a new publication, *The Autocar*, to try to attract public attention to the need to change the law. Knight had been seen on the 23rd of July driving along the Alton Road at a good 10 mph with a reporter from the *Surrey & Hants* newspaper aboard, ensuring that the deed was well reported. The authorities took no action on this occasion, but in late October when Knight and his handyman – now chauffeur – Pullinger, flagrantly drove up and down Castle Street in Farnham, they responded. Knight was charged with permitting a locomotive to be at work without a licence, and Pullinger was charged for working the same during prohibited hours – namely 3.30 p.m. The local court on 31st October, perhaps a little in awe of the local landowner, fined them both a mere 2/6d with 12/6d costs.

The hearing gave Knight the opportunity he wanted to publicise his case widely. He told the court about the recent motor show at Tunbridge Wells, how 700 cars were already on French roads and that he hoped to win a competition run by *The Engineer* magazine with a prize of 1000 guineas. Knight's car had been written up in the *Surrey & Hants* newspaper and was featured in an article in *The Engineer* which stated: "It was intended to be simply an experimental vehicle, chiefly to bring to public notice the restrictions which have hitherto prevented the use of motor carriages in England".

John Henry Knight, his son and his car 1896 *Museum of Farnham*

Knight now set about improving his vehicle, although avoiding further direct confrontation with the police. The engine cylinder and piston were enlarged to give 3 bhp; the rope transmission was replaced by leather belts and the single front wheel was replaced by two to give better stability. In May 1896 Knight's car was the only British one at the first British Motor Show at the Crystal Palace where George Parfitt gave demonstration rides. The publicity caused by Knight's court appearance and the persistent lobbying in the press and in *The Autocar* by Simms and Salomons, and particularly by the setting up of 'The Self Propelled Traffic Association' jointly by Salomons, Simms and Knight, paid off when in November 1896 Parliament passed the Locomotives on the Highways Act which raised the speed limit from 4 to 12 mph and dispensed with the need for the man with the red flag, who would have been unable anyway to run, let alone walk, at 12 mph.

An Emancipation Run from London to Brighton was held in November 1896, although there is no record of Knight actually taking part. He had bought a Benz which perhaps would have been more practical to take on the run than his own vehicle, but he appears not to have done so. This run is still held each

John Henry and Mrs Knight in their Benz 1901 *Museum of Farnham*

November and is restricted to 'Veteran' cars. Knight wrote in his 'Notes on Motor Carriages' in 1896: "English engineers will soon produce far better engines and carriages than anything our Continental neighbours have yet seen". A big statement, but certainly a new manufacturing industry was soon underway in Britain, and Surrey engineers were in the forefront.

John Henry Knight died on the 8th of September 1917 but his Trusty engine stayed in production until the end of the war in 1918, earning royalties all the time. The car was left in his will to his friend Salomons and it languished at the latter's home for many years. In 1929 the car returned to Farnham, where, after being overhauled by George Parfitt 34 years after he had built it, it ran in the carnival procession in the town. The car was then put into store by the Urban District Council until, in the nineteen fifties, the Knight family asked for it to be sent to the new Montagu Motor Museum at Beaulieu and be put on display there. It was overhauled but the engine could not be persuaded to start. In 1985 it was brought back once again to Farnham, 90 years after it was built, forming the centrepiece in a transport exhibition. Unfortunately it still could not be persuaded to run – and is unlikely now ever to do so again. Today it has a prominent position in the display at the National Motor Museum at Beaulieu.

The first British car to be driven on a public road

There has long been debate as to whether John Henry Knight's car was the first British car to be driven on a public road. For some years the contest was seen to be between Knight and Frederick Lanchester in Coventry. Neither was the first to come up with ideas, and some vehicles were built but never ran on a public road, if in fact they ran at all. In 1882 a Professor Ayrton was granted a patent for an electro-tricycle, but there is no record of it ever being built. After four years of effort, in 1887 Edward Butler built a motorised tricycle fitted with a 2 cylinder water-cooled two-stroke engine at Erith in Kent. He built a second model the next year re-designed as a four-stroke and he is said to have reported in February 1889 "that it ran reasonably satisfactorily". There is a photograph remaining of the vehicle but no record if it was truly roadworthy and capable of running on a public road.

Lanchester built a four-wheeled car at the end of 1895 and ran it in Coventry in February/March 1896. Like the Benz it was a homogeneous mechanical entity, and not a horseless carriage. The engine had a single-cylinder, was air cooled, and had two connecting rods and twin contra-rotating crankshafts. The 1.7 litre engine developed 5 hp and the car was designed to run on pneumatic tyres, the first British car to do so. In 1897 an improved engine with two cylinders was fitted, producing 10 hp. Further prototypes were developed and one of these won a gold medal at the 1899 Richmond Motor Show after running for 68 miles at an average speed of 26 mph. Production models, which followed in 1900, had a smoothness and quietness unparalleled by other contemporary cars. Epicyclic gears provided three forward gears, with preselector control of first and second. Engine and gearbox had automatic lubrication and there was worm final drive. Suspension was by cantilever springs, back and front, with steering by a side lever. The Lanchester was the first successful four-wheeled British car, as distinct from converted carriages or tricycles, owing nothing to Daimler or Benz, and was the first of the early pioneering vehicles to go into quantity production in this country.

Knight ran his three-wheeled version in July 1895, clearly pre-dating Lanchester. But his modified four-wheeler first ran in April 1896, a month or so after Lanchester. It was Knight's change from three wheels to four which seems to have confused historians.

Charles Simms must take the credit for introducing the petrol engine into Britain, when in 1891 he set up in business in an arch adjoining Putney Bridge station which he rented from the District Railway Co. He imported Daimler engines, having tried unsuccessfully to import a complete car. He was up against the British horse-loving public, and any attempt he made to oust the 'friend of man' from its position in Victorian society was met with scorn and derision. There was a real fear of the new volatile fuel and concern that the new fangled engine would cause fire and explosion and even death.

What particularly interested Simms was the Hot-Tube Ignition invented by Daimler, for it was self-timing and thus entirely automatic. The system used a tube, sealed at one end, running from the outside of the cylinder head into the combustion chamber. It was not unlike a Bunsen burner fed by its own spirit fuel supply, which played a flame on the outer end of the tube. When this glowed cherry red the engine was ready to start. Simms tried to arrange for a demonstration of the new engine at the German Exhibition which was held at Earls Court. When the authorities learnt that the fuel was some kind of highly inflammable and explosive spirit, they feared that the whole exhibition would be blown up, and refused his application.

Simms then proposed to fit the engine in a boat and demonstrate it on the Serpentine Lake in Hyde Park, again he was refused permission. He next applied to demonstrate it on the lake in the grounds of the Crystal Palace, but once again was turned down. In the end he managed to obtain permission to run his demonstration vessel on the River Thames and in the summer of 1891 his motor boat made several runs between Charing Cross and Westminster piers. Simms' experiences were reminiscent of those that Daimler himself had experienced in 1885, when the Canstatter Zeitung talked of his vehicle as being "repugnant, diabolical and dangerous to life and the well being of the citizens".

In 1912 a case was made for a then unknown engineer and plumber and son of a German immigrant, Frederick Bremer of Walthamstow. He lived in Connaught Road and had a small workshop in the back garden and had seen a Benz car which inspired him to design his own. Encouraged by his brother-in-law, Herbert Dowsing a pioneer motorist, Bremer had the parts made for him in an East London workshop. His car, in skeletal form, had its first secret road trial in December 1894. Little is known about the engine other than that it was a single cylinder, water-cooled four stroke, but who made it and how much power it produced seems not to be known.

A body was added to the car in January 1895 when further successful trials were carried out. Bremer made no attempt to publicise his work or to put the vehicle into production. Like Knight, it was a one-off built solely to satisfy his own engineering curiosity and as a personal challenge. Bremer soon lost interest once he had proved to himself that he could successfully build a car and the machine languished in the back of his workshop until he presented it to the local museum in either 1929 or 1931, records are inconsistent on the exact date. The car was withdrawn and restored in 1962 and in the autumn of 1963 the engine was coaxed back into life. The car was entered in the November 1964 Veteran Car Run to Brighton but broke down with a failed crankshaft after only 17 miles. The next year it successfully completed the run, covering the 54 miles in 7 hours and 55 minutes consuming 3 gallons of petrol, ½ a gallon of oil and 12 gallons of water. After the run the car was returned to the Vestry House Museum in Walthamstow where it remains to this day.

The Veteran Car Club subsequently upheld the claim that Frederick Bremer had in fact built and successfully run the first British car on a public road.

In the nineteen fifties news came to light of another contender, the Santler, built by the brothers Charles and William in their workshop in Malvern Link, Worcestershire. The Santlers manufactured bicycles and installed and maintained steam engines and they conceived the idea of building a car as a spare time hobby. In 1887 they built a steam-powered car, based on the two-wheeled dogcart used by sportsmen to carry their gun dogs. The engine was in a wooden box under the seat, had four wheels and was steered by a wheel on a vertical column. There were other experimental steam cars on the road at the time, so little notice would have been taken nationally of this effort, particularly as it was again built for the pleasure of it and for personal satisfaction and had no commercial potential.

What came to notice in the nineteen fifties was that apparently the Santlers subsequently to 1887 converted the engine to run on compressed coal gas, and then still later on in 1894 to petrol. Once again this car, minus its engine, languished in a shed in the Santler factory, which stayed in business until the nineteen twenties. An unnamed collector restored the vehicle in the fifties, fitting it with another engine. It disappeared again from public view until it appeared in a Christie sale catalogue in December 2001, when it was expected to fetch between £50,000 and £80,000. Since the auction the car has once again vanished into a private collection and no more is known about it. It does seem possible, I put it no higher than that, that the Santler successfully ran on a public road some time during 1894, before Bremer. But the latter is still the official holder of the British first. John Henry Knight was officially then the second with his tricycle, and Lanchester the third.

Three other important pioneering efforts must be mentioned. Herbert Austin, working at the Wolseley Sheep-Shearing Company in Birmingham, designed his tri-car based on a French Bollee design in 1896. It went into full-scale production at the end of that year, being the first British car to do so in a factory designed for the purpose. The same year, 1896, was when the Daimler Motor Syndicate was set up in Coventry by Henry Lawson, who had been involved in the cycle industry in that city. He had purchased the Daimler patents from Simms and set about building the German Daimler designs in this country. At first kits of imported parts were assembled, then complete cars built from the German designs, but by 1902 British designed cars were being made. In 1904 the trade-mark fluted radiator was adopted, whilst royal patronage had started in 1900 when the Prince of Wales, a keen motorist, took delivery of his first Daimler, a royal connection which continued into the nineteen fifties.

The third of the car manufacturing pioneers to be mentioned are the Dennis brothers of Guildford, whose story will be told in full in a subsequent chapter. Like so many others they progressed from building cycles and tricycles to fitting the latter with an engine, exhibiting their first model with a French de Dion engine at the 1899 National Cycle Show. Their first four-wheeled car appeared in 1901.

There is one more local story to be told. It is totally uncorroborated except for one reference. In 1929 a Farnham author, W Ewbank-Smith, in his book 'Farnham in War and Peace', reviewing events of that year, apparently found a reference in the Daily Sketch to a car made by a Mr. L A Durant of Rustic Walk, Lower Bourne, near Farnham. According to the paper, "Durant had given King Edward, when Prince of Wales, his very first car ride in Richmond Park in 1894. Durant had told a reporter from the Farnham Herald that this, his first car, was powered by a 2.5 hp air-cooled gas engine with a flat belt drive

46

over wooden pulleys. The chassis was made from 2" gas piping and the wheels came from two penny farthing cycles, 54" at the rear and 30" at the front".

Durant then made the remarkable claim that this vehicle was the first one ever to run on an English road. While testing in Richmond Park, he claimed that he had been hailed by Lord Knollys who introduced him to the Prince of Wales. After being given a run in Durant's car, the Prince had pinned a diamond pin to Durant's scarf, this had remained a cherished possession. Durant also claimed that he had made even earlier experiments in 1888 when he had fitted a side car to a tandem pedal cycle. He had "also assisted in C S Rolls' early experiments in a little workshop in Richmond." A remarkable story – if true. Durant may have been pulling the leg of a gullible reporter, or perhaps he suffered from delusions of power and grandeur. No one else seems to have any information on Durant's claim – he has no entry in the literature – and his strange story, including how he got the car from Bourne to Richmond Park, remains to be investigated.

The accepted story regarding the Prince of Wales and his first motor car ride is confirmed by a well-known photograph showing him at Warwick in the Daimler belonging to the present Lord Montagu's father.

Early Motoring Clubs

The Self Propelled Traffic Association was formed on the 10th December 1895. In France the Automobile Club de France had been formed a month earlier and two weeks before that the Americans had started their American Motor League with the declared aim of promoting cars "by education and agitation, by mutual defence of rights of said vehicles when threatened by adverse judicial decisions." The Self Propelled Association was a single issue pressure group with the sole intent of repealing the old Locomotives on Highway Act, the infamous 'Red Flag' Act limiting locomotives, which included the new internal combustion-engined vehicles, to 4 mph and to be preceded by a man walking in front with a red flag. The cars which had gathered at Sir David Salomons' home in Tunbridge Wells had all been capable of much higher speeds, though derisory by today's standards. Salomons was the leader of this group, which included Charles Simms, John Henry Knight, H J Lawson and Evelyn Ellis, all of whom have appeared already in our story.

47

Meeting of the Automobile Club at Knight's house at Barfield 1898 *Chris Shepheard collection*

After the successful passing of the Emancipation Act and the subsequent Emancipation Run to Brighton in November 1896, the Self Propelled Association quietly went out of existence. It was absorbed into the new Automobile Club of Great Britain and Ireland in 1897, members of which were entertained by Knight at his Farnham home on Good Friday, 1898. The Club was founded with the aim of being a 'Society of Encouragement for the motoring movement and the motor and allied industries in the British Empire, and the majority of the automobile associations in the Commonwealth associated with it'. The Club changed its title in 1907 to the Royal Automobile Club and today the RAC is the national motoring authority and a constituent member of the Federation International de l'Automobiles, which consists of the national clubs of all countries.

The Club House in Pall Mall, London was built on the site of the old War Office and opened in February 1911. In 1913 the RAC acquired Woodcote Park, Epsom, an estate of some 300 acres and of historical interest. The old Woodcote House was destroyed by fire in August 1934. A modern building was erected on the same site and was opened in June 1936. Woodcote Park, is one and a half miles from Epsom station and 16 miles by road from Hyde Park Corner.

Although the RAC may be said to have only tenuous

48

connections with Surrey, through Knight and the SPTA, and its Club House at Epsom, it can be said with certainty that the Automobile Association has much closer links. The man who inspired the formation of the AA was Charles Jarrott, a pioneer car salesman who sold American Oldsmobiles for £150 in this country. He had been convicted for 'dangerous driving' by the Lincolnshire magistrates who made their feelings clear, "cars were a disgrace and a nuisance and should be banned". They were rebuked subsequently by the Home Office who told them that they should not air their personal prejudices in public. Jarrott and his friends held a meeting in a pub and formed the Motorists Mutual Association, with the declared objective to "continue to patrol the Brighton Road as done by Charles Jarrott and to patrol other main roads as soon as subscriptions are obtained." Seventeen people joined immediately.

Soon a lone cyclist was hired to patrol the Brighton Road for five shillings a day if on foot, or four if cycling. Other patrolmen were soon appointed as funds became available. Patrolmen carried either a red handkerchief or flag or wore a rosette. Officially on duty from 8 am to dusk they were instructed to help members in trouble, they also had a duty to assist any non-member if there were injuries. Although it was never written down, to prevent the police bringing a charge of conspiracy to pervert the course of justice, the real reason for their existence was to warn members of police speed traps. Stenson Cooke, the first Secretary of the Automobile Association, put the matter as delicately as he could: "Patrols must thoroughly inspect every portion of the road which they have in their charge and be at all times ready to point out any danger which may exist to motorists."

The first executive committee of the AA included S F Edge, who was at the time General Manager of Dunlop, and Herbert Smith of what became later Smith's Industries of Putney Vale. Badges and nameplates came in 1906, as so did the famous salute. No salute, no speed trap. Interestingly when Cooke was appointed he had only been twice in a car as a passenger, and he never learnt to drive himself.

One last motoring first should be mentioned before leaving the pioneers. On the 9th June 1899 the first motor hill climb in England was held over a 325 yards course at Petersham Hill, to the west of Richmond. The entrants were mostly dealers or employees of manufacturers, but the Hon. C S Rolls averaged 8.75 mph in his racing 6 hp Panhard. So, within a very few years of the arrival of the motor car, it was being used to savour the thrill of speed.

References

The Dawn of Motoring – How the Car came to Britain: Erik Johnson, Mercedes-Benz UK Ltd.,1986

Farnham in War and Peace: W Ewbank-Smith, 1929

Local Transport – Farnham's First Car: Jonathan Wood, Farnham Museum 1985

Badshot People: Maurice Hewins, Badshot Lea Village Trust 1981

The Brooklands Story I

Building the circuit

Any consideration of motoring in Surrey must include that most famous racing circuit, airfield and major aircraft manufacturing site at Brooklands, Weybridge. In the late nineteenth century the Royal Estate of the former Oatlands Palace at Weybridge, including the land at Brooklands was bought by the Hon. Hugh Fortescue Locke King, an extremely wealthy landowner who was descended from a former Lord Chancellor of England, Baron King of Ockham. Locke King was a much travelled man and an early motoring enthusiast, as was his wife Ethel (later Dame Ethel).The idea of building a racing circuit was born after he had watched a car race through the streets of Brescia in Italy. After watching French, German and Italian cars racing round the streets in the Targo Florio race, Locke King asked, 'Why are there no English cars racing'. The reply from one of the organisers was, 'You have nowhere to practice racing in England and to develop your cars at speed. You would have no chance here'.

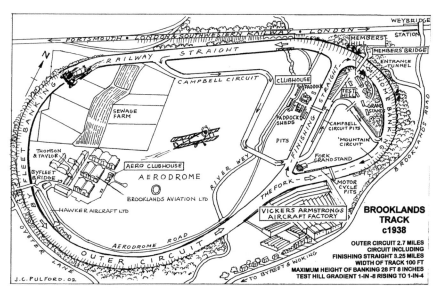

Map of Brooklands c1938 *John Pulford*

Locke King wrote to a friend after this event, "Poor old England – the cradle of sport as she used to be called and now she is nowhere. The time has surely come when England should no longer lag behind the rest of the world but take her place in the very forefront, if possible, and reassert herself as the arbiter of sport. This feeling was revived after returning home when I heard a suggestion that a circular track was what was needed in this country, where cars could be watched over the whole course. This was the only way forward as the powers that be would not sanction racing through the streets as they do in Continental Europe. The site was not far to seek. When a few who were consulted saw the place, they owned that nature seemed to have formed it for the purpose."

The law in England restricted road speeds to 20 mph in the early years of the twentieth century and there seemed little hope that it would be changed. In fact it was 1930 before it was and even then racing on public roads was not authorised. In fact it has never happened on the mainland (except for a recent experiment in Birmingham), only in Northern Ireland and on The Isle of Man has it ever been legal to close public roads for racing. Lords Northcliffe and Montagu both quickly gave support to Locke King's concept.

Locke King chose a marshy and generally unprepossessing part of his estate south west of Weybridge and across the railway from his home, Brooklands House, from which the track took its name. In the spring of 1906 some 1,500 labourers, both locals and from Ireland and Yorkshire, descended on the quiet villages of Weybridge and Byfleet and started work. Thirty acres of woodland had to be cut down and the River Wey diverted in two places from it original course. Some 30,000 cubic yards of earth were removed from a natural hillside and used to construct two giant bankings. 200,000 tons of Portland cement were used to build the track, including two tunnels, three bridges and grandstands for 30,000 spectators, with standing for another 250,000, together with access roads, restaurants and an impressive clubhouse.

A seven mile railway system was laid down connecting with the London & South Western mainline, ten steam grabs and a steam navvy were brought in as well as six traction engines, innumerable horses and carts and some 2,000 shovels for the navvies. No motor lorries appear to have been used. A circuit of 4,730 yards of concrete track was planned, incorporating an early type of ferro-concrete construction. The design was modified to include a high embankment, 28' 8" at the highest

Construction work on the circuit 1906 *Brooklands Museum*

The Hennebique bridge over the river Wey under construction 1907
Brooklands Museum

point, to facilitate high speeds. The concrete was laid 6 to 8 inches deep, and the track was 100 feet wide.

The grandstand was approached by a bridge over the track, and the club house modelled on the famous Mena House Hotel near the pyramids at Cairo, which Locke King had built and owned. The contractors were given a deadline of one year in

Mrs Locke King leading in the King's Itala on opening day 17th June1907 *Brooklands Museum*

which to complete the task. Working day and night the circuit was ready in nine months. The cost, all paid by Locke King, was £150,000. The opening day, in June 1907, was described by S F Edge, who would soon put Brooklands on the map by driving a car non-stop for 24 hours round the circuit at an average speed of 65.905 mph. "After the opening ceremony an inspection of the course was made by all present. Mr. and Mrs. Locke King (Mrs. Locke King driving) led the way in their 70 hp Itala followed by Rolls on a Rolls-Royce, J E Hutton on his 80 hp Berliet, the Duke of Westminster, Lord Lonsdale, and many others."

"I do not know what speed we were doing, but suddenly there appeared Warwick Wright on his racing Darracq. He passed us all as though we were standing still and we heard afterwards that he was touching 85 mph. It was a most enjoyable day, and congratulations were showered on Mr. and Mrs. Locke King." The tempo had been set for the next thirty-two years, until the track closed down at the start of the second World War in 1939 never to re-open.

The First Race

All the leading drivers and some of the most famous racing cars in Europe turned up for the first race meeting on 6th July 1907. The prize money was £15,000 distributed between six events, big money for the period. However the meeting was far from being a total success. Only 4,000 spectators turned up, 30,000 had been expected, and many did not seem to have enjoyed the occasion very much. The racing was dull and some of the facilities were criticised. The vastness of the circuit dwarfed the cars and robbed them of any appearance of speed. The *Surrey Herald* was not impressed,

> "On Saturday last residents of Weybridge and district adjacent to the Brooklands motor track were favoured with a foretaste of what may be expected for the next few years, or, at any rate till the public curiosity as regards the new sport dies the natural death which probably awaits it. What, after all, can there be in watching the endless circling of highly-developed machines round and round a circumscribed area?"

Before 1914

Despite the initial criticisms it was only a few years later that Locke King was approached for advice by a group of Americans who were planning to build a motor track at Indianapolis. The result of their endeavours is very much with us still. Two men who had a profound effect on the success of Brooklands arrived within two years of the opening. A V Ebblewhite, the starter and handicapper, and the Clerk of the Course, Major (later Colonel)

A V Ebblewhite, starter and handicapper *Brooklands Museum*

Lindsay Lloyd. The operation was based on horse racing even to the titles of the officials and the initial use of 'silks' to identify the drivers. 'Ebby', as he was always known, introduced the numbering of cars enabling them to be clearly identified by spectators, whilst Lloyd introduced flying to Brooklands, built the Test Hill, and above all, gave a more friendly atmosphere to the race track which it subsequently never lost.

From the beginning the track was used for events other than racing. In July 1907 the RAC organised trials to determine which type of car or tyre raised the least dust. 46 cars took part, in three

Major (later Col.) Lindsay Lloyd (left), Clerk of the Course, with Count Louis Vorow Zborowski c 1920 *Brooklands Museum*

classes. Most interest was in the third, 'experimental' class, which included such oddities as solid rubber tyres working on hollow rubber rings, and pneumatic disc wheels with the interior filled with compressed air. Fine limestone was laid down and the cars drove through 100 feet of it, first at 20 and then at 30 mph. Winners of classes 1 and 2 were both American steam cars, a White and a Stanley, a Vivinus with an undershield and a Dennis with disc wheels and undershield both received merit awards in the 'experimental' class.

Brooklands' first accident occurred during the second meeting. Huntly Walker, who had finished second in the Century Stakes, suffered brake failure when trying to slow down. He engaged reverse gear and slid up the banking. Fortunately the ground was still soft on the other side, checking the car before it reached the railings at the bottom. The driver was unharmed and ran off to prepare for the next race in another of his Darracqs. The winner of the Century Stakes was Frank Newton in a Napier, a make well represented in early races.

By 1909 other makes were making a mark. Vauxhall was a leading name right from the beginning up to the mid-twenties. They brought the first streamlined car to the track, to be followed later by many others. The Vauxhall was called 'KN', and driven by A J Hancock established a flying half-mile record of 81.33 mph. The value of streamlining was proved at the Easter meeting when 'KN' lapped at 85.24 mph compared to only 69.5 mph reached by a standard Vauxhall of the same engine size. In 1910 Hancock raised the flying half-mile record to 97 mph with 'KN', which was amended to 'Cayenne' by the press, as the car was said to be as hot as pepper!

In 1909 Hemery clocked 125.95mph in his Blitzen Benz creating a new world land speed record. In 1911 Vauxhall built a special engine to attack the 26hp records. The bore of the engine was only 80mm, bringing it into the smaller class, but the stroke was 200mm giving the engine a capacity of 4,019cc, larger than that of the 20hp cars. Hancock broke several short distance records with the car.

Another dominant make in the early years was Mercedes, due mainly to Gordon Watney who set up the South Lodge Motor Works at Weybridge, where he modified and prepared the cars. Standard bodies were replaced with doorless aluminium shells designed by him and made by the Ewart Geyser Company. He acquired some former racing cars including the Sixty with which Jenatzy had won the 1903 Gordon Bennett Race.

Apart from the Watney Mercedes cars, several other retired Grand Prix cars competed pre-1914. Among these was the 1908 Itala, which in June 1910 won the All-Comers Plate for 100 Sovereigns, driven by R Wildgoose for the owner R L T Young the brewer. The car could be fitted with a four-seat road body built by Vincents of Reading and survives in this form in the National Motor Museum at Beaulieu.

Among the curiosities running at Brooklands in the early years was the long-stroke 100mm x 250mm single cylinder Lion Peugeot with six valves. It had won at Boulogne in 1909 and the same year achieved at Brooklands a half-mile at 72.3 mph, 50 miles in 43 minutes 35 seconds and 100 miles in 87 minutes 48.5 seconds. In 1911 there was an aged de Dion Bouton 6.2 hp with a wind-cutting prow, a 10.1 hp Le Gui with a streamlined bonnet front but no body and the 14.5 hp Multi-Two which was reported as having an ear-splitting exhaust note.

From 1913 streamlining became popular. The pioneers were Vauxhall and Sunbeam plus some 'one-off' cars such as the Chenard-Walcker and the Deberitz. The latter had its radiator at the back to avoid flying stones and a man-in-the-moon face painted on the front cowl. 1909 saw W O Bentley begin his racing career with a 5hp Rex motorcycle, but he became better known for his drives in DFPs, little French cars with a streamlined body by Bentley.

One of the longest careers among Brooklands cars was the 1912 Grand Prix Lorraine-Dietrich 'Vieux Charles Troi', which was brought to the track by Malcolm Campbell. Driven by himself and Victor Hemery it broke several Class J records from 10 laps to 500 miles. Later, in 1929, the car was driven from Birmingham to Brooklands where it then went out and broke Class A records. Later still in the 1930s it raced at the Crystal Palace and in Vintage Sports Car Club events, and was still in existence in the 1990s.

In 1914 the regulations were changed for the World Land Speed Record, the mean of two runs in opposite directions was now required. Hornstead took out his Benz and set the first record under the new rules at 124.1mph. The last meeting before the war in 1914 saw two races won by Harold Lambert in his Type 13 Bugatti.

References
Brooklands, a Pictorial History: G N Georgano, 1978
The History of Brooklands Motor Course: William Boddy, 1957

CHAPTER 7

The Brooklands Story II

The Twenties

Racing restarted in 1920 and the most exciting car to appear was the large Sunbeam powered by a Manitou aircraft engine. It had shaft drive, unusual for the period when chain drive was the most popular, and its 12 cylinder engine gave 350hp at 2,000rpm. There were many surplus aircraft engines available after the war and a number of these monsters appeared on the racing scene. The Sunbeam was driven by Harry Hawker, the Australian pilot who tested for Tom Sopwith, and Kenelm Lee Guinness, who set up a new Land Speed Record in 1922 of 133.75mph, the last time that the world record was set at Brooklands. In 1920 the Sunbeam, driven by René Thomas, had broken the Gallion hill climb record. Later, in 1925, Campbell, who had bought the car from Lee Guinness and further developed it, took it to Pendine Sands in South Wales where he set a new World Land Speed Record of 146.1mph. The car has been preserved and is on display at the National Motor Museum at Beaulieu.

The leading cyclecar driver in the twenties was Archie Frazer-Nash, whose cars called 'Kim' and 'Mowgli', were his most successful. In 1920 'Kim' was built with a 1,086cc engine and chain drive. 'Mowgli' had a similar overhead camshaft engine and a lengthened wheelbase to make the car more stable on the banking. The back axle was turned into a countershaft and another axle added behind, driven by a single chain. The engine output was increased to 1,289cc. In 1926 the engine was installed in Basil Davenport's hill-climb special, 'Spider'. This car, much modified, continued to race until the eighties.

The first long-distance event to be held at Brooklands was the Junior Car Club's 200 Mile Race first run in October 1921, and was described in the *Autocar* as "the most important event of the year in Britain". The race was an easy victory for Talbot-Darracq who raced specially prepared cars whereas most of their rivals were virtually road cars with streamlined bodywork. Talbot-Darracq took the first three places, driven by Segrave, Lee

Louis Coatalen (left) and K L Guinness 1921 *Brooklands Museum*

Guinness and Campbell. Lee Guinness won again in 1922 in a similar car.

One of the most colourful figures at Brooklands after the first world war was Count Louis Vorow Zborowski. Born of a Polish father and an American mother, he had owned a Watney Mercedes before the war, and in 1921 he built the first of his monster cars which he used for both touring and racing, and which were known as the 'Chitty-Chitty-Bang-Bangs'. Yes there really were cars of that name, they were not merely later dreamed up by Hollywood. The first car had a 23 litre 6-cylinder German Maybach aero engine developing some 300bhp, and was mounted in a pre-war 75hp chain-driven Mercedes Chassis, with a simple open four-seat body by Blythe Brothers of Canterbury. Zborowski wore the 'regulation' check cap back-to-front as did all his team and many of his supporters. The car was later fitted with a two-seat body and an engine cowl. Zborowski crashed the car badly in 1922 and it was eventually broken up. Two further 'Chittys' were built, one of which survives.

Another Zborowski car was the 21.5 litre Blitzen Benz, believed to be the same car in which Hemery set up the world land speed record in 1909. In 1922 the car won the 100mph Long Handicap race and came second in the 100mph Short Handicap. The Benz had a one to one top gear ratio.

Zborowski was not only interested in monster cars but in the more typical type of racer as well. He approached Aston Martin and drove for them in the 1921 200 mile race. This led to considerable financial backing for the small firm which only ended with the tragic death of the Count when driving his Mercedes during the 1924 Italian Grand Prix.

Captain, later Sir, Alistair Miller drove a variety of cars. His first outing at Brooklands was in 1920 driving a 1914 Grand Prix Opel. He later drove Wolseley 'Moths' with 2 or 2.8 litre engines, becoming the competitions manager for the firm in 1921 and 1922. He also drove the Wolseley 'Viper' which had by contrast an 11,727cc Hispano-Suiza aero engine fitted into an old Napier chassis. Although it was said to be the most dangerous car at Brooklands at the time, Miller never crashed it. The car was also driven by Kaye Don, who, in 1922, lapped the circuit at 112.68mph.

In 1928 Delage closed down their competitions department and Miller bought two of their large 6 cylinder engined cars. One, driven by René Thomas, had success on continental hill climb events, but the cars were difficult to maintain and did not have a very successful career at Brooklands under Miller.

Another of the giant cars powered by ex aero engines, which rivalled the Chittys and the Viper, was the Isotta-Maybach, built by Ernest Eldridge in 1922 and which used a 20.5 litre 6 cylinder Maybach engine in a lengthened 1907 Isotta-Fraschini chassis. In 1923 it was bought by L C G M le Champion who fitted a streamlined tail and lapped Brooklands in it at 114.75mph. One of le Champion's tricks was to burst worn-out tyres by skidding the car on the aerodrome tarmac. Motor racing in the twenties was a devil-may-care game, with numerous pranksters among the more serious drivers.

AC were regular competitors in the twenties and fielded five cars in the 1921 200 Mile Race. Three had 1.5 litre Anzani engines, the other two were fitted with John Weller's 2 litre Six, which was to be come one of the longest lasting engines in any make of car. It was continually developed until after the end of the second world war. Sammy Davis was the top AC driver, he created many class and distance records for the marque in the twenties. It was customary at this time to still carry a riding mechanic, those on the Weller-engined ACs had a busy time, with two hand pumps to operate, one to scavenge and one to feed fresh oil to the engine.

In 1922 S F Edge set out to break his own 24 hour records set with the Napier fifteen years previously. Edge, an Australian, was Managing Director of AC but his firm could not provide a suitable car so he bought a Dutch Spiker for his attempt. As racing at night was not allowed, he had to make his attempt in two 12 hour stages. He easily beat his previous record of 65.91mph with a new figure of 74.27mph, at the same time capturing no less than 30 Class G records. Edge was in radio contact with his mechanic throughout his attempt, the first time that it had been used on a race track.

Morgan three-wheelers were regular competitors in light car events until they were banned in 1925 following an accident in the 1924 200 Mile Race. One of the most well-known Morgan drivers was E B Ware, who formerly rode Zenith motorcycles and was employed by JAP, the engine makers.

Lanchester was not thought of as a sporting make but at least three ran at Brooklands. Tommy Hann's extraordinary 1911 25hp model ran as a saloon in 1921 and re-appeared as an open single-seater in 1922. There were two 'Forties', the first had a two-seater body and a slightly tuned engine and was entered in 1921 by C A Bird, son of the custard manufacturer. Later S F Edge tried to cover a thousand miles within twelve hours, only giving up when George Lanchester noticed that a wheel was wobbling and feared steering failure on his 'Forty'. Edge said that the Lanchester was the most comfortable car he had ever driven, bumps on the track being hardly noticeable, even at 100mph. In 1924 the 'Forty' was driven by Parry Thomas,

George Duller and Lionel Rapson in successful attempts on Class G records. Between 1924 and 1926 the single-seater racer achieved seven firsts, mostly driven by Parry Thomas.

Among the smallest cars to seen on the track were the Jappic and the Avon-Jap, both designed to attack records in the smallest classes rather than for racing. The Jappic, designed by H M Walters and built at Wimbledon, was powered by a 344cc vertical single cylinder JAP motor-cycle engine driving the rear axle by a single chain. In 1925 Walters took all the Class J records from 1 to 10 miles, and the standing and flying start kilometre records, the latter at 70.46mph. With Kaye Don driving and with a 495cc engine the car took several Class I records as well.

The Avon-JAP, also driven by Don and fitted with a 495cc engine took Class I records which stood until the track closed. With 731cc and 968cc engines he also held Class G and H records until they were taken from him by drivers of Austin, MG and Riley cars in the thirties. The Austin Seven was a familiar sight from 1924 through to 1939. In 1924 E C Gordon England introduced his 'Brooklands' model with twin Zenith carburetors and a streamlined aluminium body with a pointed tail. It could reach 75mph and cost only £295 to build. They were mainly driven by private owners, such as Hendy, Waite, Hall and Depper.

The first supercharged Seven was built in 1925 and raced by Waite and Duller. Next came the celebrated 'Ulster' model, named after its success in the 1929 Ulster TT. One car, driven by Sammy Davis and the Earl of March, won the 1930 500 mile race at 83.42mph.

The British Grand Prix at Brooklands

It is not well-known, except to the aficionado, that the first two British Grand Prix were held at Brooklands in 1926 and 1927. Victory by Major Henry Segrave in France in 1923 and in San Sebastian in 1924, driving a Talbot-Darracq on each occasion, kindled interest at home for a British Grand Prix. Added to this Segrave, Campbell and Parry Thomas had all broken the world land speed record for Britain during the previous 18 months. Britain was thought to be favourite for the European Grand Prix in 1925 but it was eventually awarded to Belgium, the RAC, after some deliberation, awarded the 1926 race to Brooklands. Thus the first British Grand Prix was held on 7 August 1926 attracting an international field such had never been seen before in Britain.

The entry list was 13 cars, including the straight-eight 1.5 litre Delages and Talbot-Darracqs from France. Local entries were Campbell in a Bugatti, Eyston in an Aston Martin, Halford in his Special and two Thomas Specials which did not start due to gear box problems. Fiat and Alvis were the only major manufacturers not present due to changes in the regulations which did not now suit their cars so well. Startled by the speeds that the two litre cars were achieving, the officials had changed the rules now restricting power to 1.5 litres and the minimum weight reduced from 1,433lbs to 1,322lbs. Alfa Romeo were not represented either, they were resting on their laurels for the time being.

Responding to criticisms that the track was a far cry from a road circuit, the RAC instructed that two artificial earth banks, or chicanes, be constructed. One just after the pits and the other on the gradient where the straight rose to meet the final section on the Members' Banking. Even so the course was hardly a challenge when compared to San Sebastian or Spa.

New pits were built on the finishing straight and a bridge erected linking the paddock with the public enclosure. The fact that one of the bridge supports was on the track itself caused some alarm, but packing it around with sandbags seemed to reduce the drivers' fears. 'Ebby' Ebblewhite raised his red flag to start the race at 2 pm. The starters, now down to nine, roared away and the first British Grand Prix was under way. After 4 hours and 56 seconds of racing at an average 71mph it was surprising that any survived. The Delages suffered from overheating but the one driven by Senechal and Wagner was the winner, followed by Campbell's Bugatti some ten minutes behind, and the Benoist and Dubonnet Delage a further eight minutes away. They were the only finishers, the Talbot-Darracqs who had been expected to do well all gave trouble of one sort or another and retired. "Three different leaders in thirteen laps," the *Autocar* reported, "augured a real race".

The overheating of the Delages was more than a problem for the cars, the drivers too suffered badly. The exhaust passed along the right-hand side of the car and soon the body panels were scorched, as were the driver's feet, as the pedals became like hot-plates. Worse for Senechal, his exhaust box split and he drove in agony. When he stopped on the eightieth lap, he limped from the car, the soles of his shoes burned right through, and plunged his feet into a pan of cold water, an accessory which had become a vital part of the Delage pit equipment.

Wagner, with some reluctance, took over again, for he too had badly burned his feet earlier in the race, and drove to the end. Benoist was in similar trouble, the pan was refilled with cold water and Dubonnet was asked to take over the car which was running in second place at the time. Dubonnet had never driven round the circuit before and for good measure was wearing a blue lounge suit and beret as he climbed into the Delage. Segrave in a Talbot-Darracq had led the race in the early stages until he retired with engine problems leaving Divo in a similar car to fight it out with the Delages. But he too retired when his supercharger casing ruptured.

One of the few specials which competed on reasonably equal terms with the factory-built cars was the Halford built by Major Frank Halford. It was Frank's son who became the 'H' in HRG which set up on the Kingston by-pass in the thirties to build 'traditional' sports cars in the Frazer-Nash style, (see chapter 11). The Halford had a 1.5 litre twin ohc 6-cylinder engine designed by the Major. It was fitted with aluminium pistons and a Roots-type blower which gave the engine some 96bhp compared with 90bhp from Campbell's Type 37A Bugatti and 108bhp from the Talbot-Darracqs, The chassis and gearbox was made by Aston Martin, redesigned to cope with the increased engine output. The Halford had won several short races earlier in 1926 and was holding fourth place in the Grand Prix until forced out with a broken universal joint on the eighty second lap.

Although *The Motor* described the Grand Prix as "one of he most extraordinary races that has ever been run", the newspapers were not impressed. The next day the Daily Sketch gave a brief report and a single picture under the heading 'Red Hot Racing', giving far more coverage to the horse racing at Lewes. The Daily News carried on its front page an advertisement – "The British Grand Prix won on British petrol. For Acceleration, Speed and Power, use BP". The report by 'Chiltern' in the Daily News was not even on the sports pages, but alongside the City news and advertisements for State Express cigarettes at ten for sixpence (2.5p), and a Ford motor car for £125. Perhaps the *Motor* comment better summed up the enthusiasts' feelings, "Yes! We have had our Grand Prix at last and a wonderful race it has been".

A month after the Grand Prix came the 200 Mile Race, competitors in the 1.5 litre class included many of the Grand Prix contenders. Three Talbot-Darracqs were entered, again driven by Segrave, Divo and Moriceau. They lead the race for most of the time until Moriceau skidded and went off. Segrave won the race, his third '200' victory, with Divo second, thus somewhat redeeming the team following their poor showing the month before.

The 1927 British Grand Prix was also held at Brooklands, being the last in this country until after the 1939-45 war, although two races were held at Donnington in 1937 and 1938 which were of such quality that they were awarded a 'Grand Prix' title although the RAC did not see fit to confer the prefix 'British'. The entry list in 1927 showed sixteen cars, which looked promising, but again it did not work out that way. The second Grand Prix at Brooklands proved to be an even more tedious event than the first. There had been much activity in the factories of the major teams to take advantage of the modified formula. The minimum weight was raised from 1,322lb to 1,543lb and drivers were now allowed to be seated centrally in the cockpit. Riding mechanics had been banned the previous year, but the cars had remained two-seaters.

Bugatti improved their engine performance. Talbot-Darracq strengthened the front axles and made other minor changes while Delage made a major change to their engine design. By altering the cylinder head porting they were able to redirect the exhaust along the nearside of the car and away from the driver's feet. The revised straight eight engine now gave an official 170bhp but everyone knew that to be a conservative figure.

Six Bugattis were entered, including three works entries for Louis Chiron, Emilio Materassi and Count Conelli. A private entry was shared between George Eyston and Sammy Davis and Prince Ghika drove his own car. Malcolm Campbell again entered his privately owned Type 39. Three works Delages were entered, driven by Benoist, Bourlier and Divo. A pair of Thomas Specials were entered but the team was struggling to survive without their guiding light, Parry Thomas. Alvis and Fiat again withdrew, the latter because they were concentrating on developing their aero engines for the Schneider Trophy Race. Café talk at Brooklands however said that the real reason was that they had only managed to build one race car and were fearful of taking on the mighty Delage team with only the one car.

Apart from slightly easing the chicanes, the circuit was the same as for the previous year's event. The field of eleven eventual starters crumbled away during the 326 miles of racing. Both the Thomas Specials went out with clutch and transmission problems, the Bugatti of Materassi gushed out water from a fractured radiator whilst that of Eyston and Davis had a seized supercharger and Campbell paid the price for running with smaller brakes to accommodate his preference for wire wheels, while Prince Ghika's car suffered from a gasket failure. Unlike the previous year all was serene in the Delage pits. With the race going totally their way the drivers were ordered to slow down and Divo, who had lead for most of the race, was called in to attend to what seemed to be a perfectly sound exhaust. This allowed Benoist to sweep into the lead, a fitting place for the European Champion. Divo then rejoined the race for the final lap giving the Delage team a clean sweep with first, second and third places.

The journalists did not know what to write. 'Chiltern' in the 'Daily News' set to with a vengeance. Under the heading of "Motor Race Fiasco", he wrote: "Thousands of motor enthusiasts visited Brooklands in the rain on Saturday to see a race for the British Car Grand Prix, with a prize of £1,000 to the winner, £300 to the second man and £200 to the third. What they saw was a travelling car 'mannequin' parade demonstrating the high-speed reliability of French engines and cars, a free gift of world prestige from the British trade.

"The three Delages, contemptuously indifferent to the other machines on the track, ran the race as if they were tied together like camels in a convoy, 200 yards between each, two of the cars changing places near the end. The race travesty was won by E Benoist (Delage), with E Bourlier (Delage) second and A Divo (Delage) third. Benoist, in winning four out of five world championship Grands Prix in one year has created a record which will stand for many years. [Today this looks small beer compared to Michael Schumacher's results, although is four from five perhaps as good as ten from twelve].

"The only thing the British trade has to pride itself on in the race is that the three Delages were all fitted with British tyres, which were the only thing upholding British motor prestige is this so-called British Grand Prix. The ignoring by the British car trade of Saturday's racing gave the French makers the right to tell the world that they are supreme in high-speed reliable motor cars, whereas they are not, for British brains, British workmen and British drivers can beat them if given the chance by the makers."

'Chiltern' was a serious and respected motoring journalist, so in view of the patriotism prevailing at the time his report was bound to have an effect on the immediate future of Grand Prix racing in Britain and it marked the beginning of a low period in the sport as the governing body dithered over suitable regulations for the next few years. It undoubtedly influenced the RAC in its decision not to support plans for future British Grand Prix, it was not until after 1945 that their attitude changed.

A note on the first-aid arrangements at Brooklands at the time illustrates the general low-key approach to safety. Charles Mortimer, who raced there during the twenties and thirties, looking back, recalled in his memoirs, "The majority of Brooklands staff were fairly elderly, there was a delightful old gentleman called 'Iodine Walker' whose main duties were the maintenance of the lavatories – and first aid. Walker was absolutely fearless and supremely confident in all matters concerning first aid – he would tackle any injury, however serious, with an air of confidence that calmed everybody. His resources as regards equipment seemed extremely limited, even to us, but he made up for this by the lavish use of iodine which he seemed able to acquire in ten-gallon drums. Walker used iodine in the treatment of the most unusual injuries – but everyone survived and it was generally agreed that in the matter of first-aid, Walker knew what he was doing!"

J G Parry Thomas

If ever a driver deserved the title of a Brooklands habitué it was Parry Thomas who lived in a bungalow at the track from 1923 until his death in 1927. He deserves a spot all to himself in the Brooklands story. John Godfrey Parry Thomas was a big, shy man, often looking sullen in photographs, but was actually rather sociable and particularly popular with the children of his married friends, though he himself never married.

He was born in 1885 in Wrexham, North Wales, and was educated at Oswestry School and the City and Guilds Engineering College in London. From 1905 to 1907 he worked as an apprentice at Siemens Brothers & Co. Ltd. and at Clayton and Shuttleworth Ltd. At the end of 1907, aged only 22, he set up his own business, financed by his mother, to work on experimental electric transmissions for motor vehicles. He subsequently set up Thomas Transmissions Ltd., with Hedley Thomson and W F Hickman, and then Thomas Foreign Patents Ltd. Parry Thomas needed workshops for heavy component machining and approached Leyland Motors who agreed to provide him with space and fitters. Electrical work was carried out by Dick Kerr Ltd., later English Electric, at Preston. By 1914 the transmission was perfected, it worked perfectly but proved too expensive to be practical.

During the war Parry Thomas worked as an advisor to the Government on the development of aero engines and in 1917 joined Leyland as Chief Engineer. Here he set about designing the perfect motor car from scratch. He was one of those men who did everything himself, the word 'delegate' was unknown to him. He produced the famous Leyland Eight which was the sensation of the 1920 Motor Show at Olympia, the chassis alone cost £2,500. The engine was of 6,967cc and was rated as 40 hp for tax purposes. Features which placed it ahead of rivals included an oil tank which fed the gearbox by gravity and an automatic chassis lubricating system.

Altogether 14 Leyland Eight cars were built, several were sold to Indian Maharajahs, and one to Michael Collins the Irish politician. Had Leyland tooled up to build the cars in quantity then prices could have been reduced, but at the time only millionaires could afford the car. The model appeared for the last time at the 1923 Motor Show as Leyland decided not to continue with the car in order to concentrate on building commercial vehicles and buses.

At the end of 1921 Parry Thomas had persuaded the directors to allow him to enter a Leyland Eight for the Brooklands Easter Monday meeting the following year. They reluctantly agreed, provided that the car was a two-seater on the short 'Speed Model' chassis and was fitted with a full touring body. They were not to know that once the car was at the track Parry Thomas would strip off every unnecessary accessory, and even some that should have remained. The line up for the race included Campbell and Zborowski on Ballots, Coatalen in the 12-cylinder Sunbeam, a Talbot-Darracq, a Vauxhall, a Lorraine-Dietrich and the Viper, eleven cars in all. Despite his complete lack of experience Parry Thomas was not overawed, unfortunately the Leyland had clutch trouble forcing an early retirement from the race, not an auspicious start.

The car was entered in further races during 1922 but found no real success until, after major modifications were made to the suspension which improved its handling, Parry Thomas' first well-deserved win came in the 30th 100mph Short Handicap Race over 5.75 miles. He won with an average speed of 94.25mph, and touched 103.11mph on the straight. The car was then fitted with a pointed tail and the bonnet rounded off behind the radiator, with these modifications the car was very successful. At the end of his first season Parry Thomas had achieved three firsts, eight seconds and three thirds, proving his worth both as a designer and a driver. He had no mishaps, no misjudgements, just steadily improving success.

At the start of the 1923 season Parry Thomas settled into 'The Hermitage', a bungalow alongside the track at Brooklands, with Kenneth Thomson, who he had met at the City and Guilds, and who later set up Thomson and Taylor, builders of many famous race cars at Brooklands (see appendix II). Leyland Motors had been very understanding during 1922 but the time had come for a decision. Parry Thomas could either be Chief Designer for Leyland or a racing driver, but not both. His contract was mutually terminated and several complete Leyland Eight chassis and all the available spares were acquired by Parry Thomas.

First a similar car to that raced by Parry Thomas was prepared for Capt. J E P Howey, who raced it at Brooklands and elsewhere but without the success of Parry Thomas. Then Parry Thomas met T B André who had taken over the building in Weybridge of the British version of his French designed car, known over here as the Marlborough. They co-operated in building a racing version known as the Marlborough-Thomas, fitting it with a larger engine of 1,982cc capacity developed from a design intended for use in London Taxis. The engine had many Leyland characteristics, including overhead camshafts and valves controlled by leaf springs.

The car was raced by André and others without great success, but Parry Thomas in the Leyland continued his winning ways. The 2nd June meeting in 1923 saw Parry Thomas in four events, winning three of them. Unlike modern races, where all entrants are of similar design and power, cars of various power and potential speed were entered in the early races, and the ability of Ebblewhite as handicapper was essential in ensuring exciting but fair races. Following each win the Leyland received further handicapping but it did not prevent Parry Thomas winning. In the Essex Senior 100mph race he was put back from scratch to minus 13 seconds, this proving just too much. According to the race report, "he drove at a tremendous pace, but it was to no avail".

It was at the BARC summer meeting on 23rd June that Parry Thomas made a mark in Brooklands history. In the 10th Lightning Long Handicap race varying sorts of trouble had overtaken all the competitors except the Leylands of Parry

Ernest Eldridge in his 27,714cc FIAT 'Mephistopheles' leading Parry Thomas in his Leyland on the Byfleet banking 1924 *Brooklands Museum*

Thomas and Howey. The latter was in front for most of the race, but Parry Thomas, without a tread left on either of his rear tyres, swept past almost on the line to win at an average speed of 115.25mph, the fastest race to date at Brooklands.

During the winter the car was redesigned and emerged in 1924 as the Leyland-Thomas No 1 with a much lower body and a long pointed tail. A circular radiator was behind a new oval opening, whilst a redesigned crankshaft gave a raised compression ratio of 7.5:1 and the engine now produced 200bhp at 2,800rpm. Four Zenith carburetors were fitted. The car was painted white with the chassis and disc wheels in blue. It was to become the most successful car that the track had known and in the three years from 1924 to 1926 it won fifteen races, nearly all of them handicaps in which it was forced to work up the field from scratch. After Thomas' death the car was raced by W B Scott until 1930 when it was fitted with a four-seater Vanden Plas touring body.

In 1925–26 Parry Thomas worked on something at the other end of the scale from the Leyland-Thomas. These were the 1.5 litre Thomas Specials, the 'flat irons', so called because of their small frontal area and height. It was said that they were so low that the cars could run upside down as the top of the wheels were higher than the car. Two were built for the 1926 British Grand Prix, but failed to start. On 8th October, in what turned out to be Parry Thomas's last race at Brooklands, he won a 50 Mile

Handicap Race in one of the 'Flat Irons'. They were subsequently raced until 1932 by Harold Purdy and W B Scott.

Parry Thomas now turned to speed trials, racing at Saltburn sands, where he came third behind Campbell in his Sunbeam and Eldridge in his huge Fiat. On 4th October Parry Thomas was racing at the Montlhéry circuit outside Paris when news came of the death of Count Zborowski driving the new supercharged Mercedes in the Italian Grand Prix at Monza. When the Count's cars subsequently came up for sale Parry Thomas bought, for £125, the Higham Brooklands Special, named after the Count's Kent home. It spent a long time in the Brooklands workshops finally emerging as 'Babs', the best remembered of the Parry Thomas cars.

It retained the 27 litre Liberty aero engine in the pre-war Mercedes chassis but was now fitted with a typical Thomas long pointed tail, not unlike the Leyland-Thomas in appearance. Although the car was mostly driven by Parry Thomas he allowed John Cobb to take the car out on a few occasions. Why 'Babs'? As far as we know Parry Thomas never had a girl friend named 'Babs', or one of any other name. Some say it was just a popular name of the period, or a corruption of 'Baby' which had been written on the car by a mechanic impressed by its size, but the most likely reason is that it was named after the small daughter of his good friend Archie Frazer-Nash. This has been subsequently confirmed by the lady in question although in recent years two other claimants have made their case in correspondence with the Brooklands Museum.

The car was raced at Brooklands but it was more at home when running flat out on the sands at Pendine in South Wales where Parry Thomas in April 1926 took the world land speed record at 169.30mph, raising it later in the year to 171.02mph. In December 1926 Campbell took his new Napier-Campbell, his first 'Bluebird' built for record breaking as distinct from racing, to Pendine. It was designed by Reid Railton and built for him by Thomson and Taylor at Brooklands. Watched by Parry Thomas, a trial run showed that all was not well with the gearbox. After remedial work was completed on the gearbox Campbell returned to Pendine on 2nd January 1927 when in poor conditions he achieved 172.86mph in one direction, touching 176mph for a short distance, but the record stayed with 'Babs'.

On 4th February 1927 Campbell took the record at a mean speed of 174.883mph and on a further set of runs took it up to 179.158mph. Parry Thomas had spent the winter working on

Malcolm Campbell in his Napier Campbell on Pendine Sands 1926
National Motor Museum

'Babs' and was determined to regain the record. There was urgency for Sunbeam had built a huge twin-engined 1,000hp car, designed by Louis Coatalen, for Segrave to drive, and now that the US had joined the International Association of Recognised Automobile Clubs, world records made across the Atlantic would be recognised. Segrave was off to Florida where there were much longer beaches available than anywhere in Britain. Parry Thomas returned to Pendine, in spite of still recovering from influenza, and on 3rd March 1927, in poor weather conditions, made a fast first run. The plugs were changed and carburettor settings adjusted and Parry Thomas set off on the return run.

Major Callingham, Thomas's technical advisor, drove down the side of the course to warn the timekeepers to expect 'Babs'. Before he was clear of the measured mile 'Babs' flew past him in a cloud of spray, sand and exhaust. Callingham next saw flames and black smoke and rushing down the beach he was met by a horrifying sight. 'Babs' had swung round and was facing out to sea. The near-side front wheel was at an angle while the off-side one had vanished and the engine was on fire. Poor Parry Thomas was lying half out of the cockpit, the top of his head completely taken off by the whip of the broken driving chain. The sad news spread a heavy gloom over Pendine.

At the inquest next day it was agreed that the driving chain must have broken and struck the driver, killing him instantly. The cause of the breakage was never officially known, one theory at the time was that Parry Thomas had lifted his foot at the end of the mile before declutching, causing the chain to ride up on the driving sprocket and break. Another theory was that a front tyre burst overturning the car at high speed, but photographs seemed to dispute this.

But the most likely theory was put forward by Reid Railton who had carefully inspected the remains of 'Babs' and found that one tooth of the driving wheel sprocket had an indentation that could have only been caused by something harder than the steel from which the sprocket was made. The only harder steel was that used for the wheel spokes. Trying a piece of broken spoke in the dent, he found that it fitted perfectly. Railton concluded that the off-side wheel had collapsed at speed, it being well-known that wire wheels did not stand up well to the snatch of chain-drive, and that a piece of broken spoke had lodged between the chain and the chain-wheel breaking the chain as a result. With full power on the driving sprocket, the free length of chain would fly upwards, while at the same time the car would heel over in the direction of the collapsed wheel, flinging Parry Thomas towards the flying chain.

A proposal to tow the car out to sea was not taken up and 'Babs' was buried in the dunes in a hole seven feet deep. The engine was destroyed to discourage souvenir hunters. Parry Thomas's leather coat was cut into pieces and together with the remains of his helmet was also put into the hole. Parry Thomas's body was taken back to the 'Hermitage' where a private service was held on 7th March. He was then taken through the paddock to be buried in the churchyard of St. Mary's, Byfleet. There was a large gathering at the funeral and his goggles were laid to rest with him. Subsequently a granite stone with a large black cross was erected at the head of his grave bearing the following words including a quotation from a prayer by Bishop Brent:

JOHN GODFREY PARRY THOMAS
Born 6th April 1885
Accidentally killed on Pendine Sands
when attempting World's Motor Speed Record
3rd March 1927
Life is eternal and love is immortal
and death which is only the horizon is
nothing save the limit of our sight.

Over the years there were rumours that an attempt was to be made to dig up the car. But the land became Crown Property and after the Second World War became part of an experimental rocket range so it would have been virtually impossible. However forty-two years later, in 1969, permission was granted and 'Babs' was exhumed, in a bad condition but still recognisable. She was taken to North Wales where Owen Wyn Owen started on the long road to restoring her, initially planned only as a static exhibit. But with support from British industry, and the fortuitous discovery of a brand new Liberty engine in New York, the car was restored to full running condition. The only non-standard fitting was a chain guard over the otherwise exposed driving chain. The task was completed in 1985 when she went on display in Wrexham, Parry Thomas' birthplace.

In May 1995 'Babs' was driven again at the 'Brooklands Action Day' held at the Millbrook proving ground, the motor industry test track in the Midlands, driven by Wyn Owen's son, Dr. G Owen. She then went on display in her own museum in 1996 at Pendine, where she can be seen during the summer months. The car ran again in public making a demonstration run at the Goodwood Festival of Speed in June 1997, again driven by Dr. Owen. In March 1997 'Babs' had been on display at Brooklands, part of a 'Memorial Tour' from Pendine. From February to May 1998 the car was displayed at the National Motor Museum at Beaulieu and was back again at Brooklands in 2001. She is now at Brooklands regularly over the winter months.

The car has also appeared again more recently at the Goodwood Festival and it is fitting that once more the roar of that mighty Liberty engine can still occasionally be heard to remind us of John Godfrey Parry Thomas.

References
Brooklands, a Pictorial History: G N Georgano, 1978
The History of Brooklands Motor Course: William Boddy, 1957
The History of Motor Racing: William Boddy, 1978
Delage Ascendant: Rupert Prior, The Spirit – The Brooklands Magazine, 1996
The Brooklands Greats – J G Parry Thomas: John Granger, The Spirit – The Brooklands Magazine, 2001

CHAPTER 8

The Brooklands Story III

The Thirties

Malcolm Campbell gave up racing in the mid-thirties to concentrate on record breaking. His first drive at Brooklands had been in 1911 and his last was in 1935. The first car given the name 'Bluebird' by him was a 1906 10.5 litre Darracq with which Campbell had won at the 1912 June meeting. He drove Talbot, Itala, Austro-Daimler, Ballot and Chrysler cars before he was caught up in a wave of enthusiasm for record-breaking in 1924. His last racing mount in the thirties was a 4 litre V-12 Sunbeam. In February 1928 he had taken his Thomson and Taylor re-built Napier-Campbell 'Bluebird', now with more powerful Napier Lion engines, to Daytona where he set a new record of

Campbell and Bugatti in pits 1930 *Brooklands Museum*

76

Campbell's Mercedes 38/250 outside Campbell Shed 1931 *Brooklands Museum*

206.956mph, eclipsing the 203.792 mph set in March 1927 by Segrave in the giant Sunbeam, also at Daytona. From 1929 Campbell worked on up-grading 'Bluebird' and in February 1931 took back the record at 246.09mph which he had lost again to Segrave in 1929, the latter now driving the beautiful Napier Lion-engined 'Golden Arrow'. Campbell raised the record once more to 253.97mph in February 1932.

'Bluebird' was again re-designed for 1933 and re-built once more by Thomson and Taylor at Brooklands with a Gurney Nutting body. In February Campbell raised the record to 272.46mph, again at Daytona beach. In 1934 'Bluebird' received its final re-build and was fitted with a Rolls-Royce 'R' engine, based on the one designed for the Schneider Trophy seaplane races, and fitted with a streamlined body with a stabilising fin. In March 1935 Campbell raised the record to 276.82mph. He was determined to be the first to break the 300mph barrier, he had been beaten to the 200mph mark by Segrave in 1927, and now took his car to the Bonneville salt flats in Utah where, in September 1935, he took the record past the magic 300 mark to 301.129mph. On his return to Britain he was knighted for breaking the record five times in as many years. Much of the technical success of the record-breaking 'Bluebirds' must be credited to Leo Villa, Campbell's brilliant but eccentric mechanic.

The last 'Bluebird' is the car those of us of a certain age

remember, and of which we probably had a 'Dinky' model. Unlike 'Babs', we know how the 'Bluebirds' got their name. The cars were always painted a bright blue colour and were named after a long-running and popular play in a West End theatre at the time the first one was driven by Campbell. It is sometimes asked why the earlier record-breaking 'Bluebirds' were not retained, preserved and displayed. In fact each successive 'Bluebird' was a re-build of the previous one. So only the final example remains, albeit now in poor condition due to the ravages of time and the Bonneville salt, in the Alabama Speedway Hall of Fame in Utah, U.S.A. A glass-fibre replica is in the Windermere museum in the Lake District. There were rumours in the late 1990's that the car was being brought back to Britain to be restored by the Thrust Organisation at Farnborough, but it has not yet come to pass.

Meanwhile back at Brooklands, Austin in 1931 built a single-seater with the express purpose of regaining the Class H records which Eyston in his MG had captured. The car had been wind-tunnel tested and was more streamlined than previous versions. Poppe was the driver in its first event, from which it was retired. Later Leon Cushman attacked the two-way kilometre record breaking Eyston's speed with 102.28mph. When Gwenda Stewart, one of a number of lady drivers now racing competitively with the men, attained over 100mph at Montlhéry, Austin built a team of four cars, converting the record-breaking car to the same specification. They were known as the 'rubber ducks' due to their squat appearance. The full team ran in the 1931 500 mile race.

The giant cars, such as the 21.5 litre Benz, competed through the twenties until in 1930 they were banned as were all chain-driven machines, on safety grounds. Long distance events became popular, inspired by the growing influence of Le Mans. Six hour events for sports cars in road trim were organised as at Le Mans. Cars were set a minimum distance to cover depending on their power, the one exceeding it by the biggest margin in each class was awarded a gold medal. In the first race Bentleys were the first three home, the outright distance winner of the Essex Club Gold Cup was Ramoni in his Alfa-Romeo. The second greatest margin was Dingle in his Austin Seven, winning the 750cc class. Peacock's Riley Nine won the 1,000cc class in the model's first race.

The Brooklands Automobile Racing Club (BARC) took over organisation of the six hour race. As the cars had to cover a set minimum mileage according to the engine capacity, it became a distance rather than an endurance event. In May 1931 the third Junior Car Club (JCC) Double Twelve Hours Race took place, run from 8.00 am to 8.00 pm on successive days, the cars being kept locked in the paddock overnight. Fewer larger cars than previously were entered but there were 24 MG Midgets and 10 Austin Sevens taking part. The race was won by an Austin Seven driven by the Earl of March and Chris Staniland.

Sammy Davis had a nasty accident in the 1931 Easter Mountain Handicap Race when his 4.5 litre Invicta slid down the banking and overturned breaking his leg in two places. Whilst in hospital he wrote his classic book 'Motor Racing'. Several 30/98 Vauxhalls competed with distinction at Brooklands, the best known, and the fastest, was R J Munday's OE-Type four-seater. Its best result was in 1932 when it won the Gold Star Handicap lapping at 114.23mph. In 1933 he put the engine into a 1922 Sunbeam chassis, the resulting Munday Special running until 1935.

One of the most famous of the Outer Circuit cars in the thirties was the 4.5 litre 'Blower' Bentley that had been built for the 1929 500 Mile Race. For 1930 it was fitted with a single-seat body designed by Reid Railton, and driven by Sir Henry Birkin it set a new lap record of 135.33mph. Two year's later the same combination raised it to 137.96mph. Its last race at Brooklands was

Clive Dunfee's fatal accident on the Members' banking in his Bentley during the BRDC 500 mile race 1932 *SIHG collection*

the famous challenge for 100 Sovereigns with John Cobb in his V-12 Delage, which Birkin won by one fifth of a second, or 25 yards.

Another famous Bentley was the Barnato Hassan, built by Wally Hassan for Woolf Barnato. It appeared in 1934 and was basically the engine from Barnato's 6.5 litre 'Old Number One' mounted in a slim chassis underslung at the rear, with a single-seat offset as the steering wheel had not been centred. It retired in the 500 Mile Race and re-appeared in 1935, having been taken over by Oliver Bertram who fitted an 8 litre engine. In August 1935 Bertram took the Outer Circuit record at 142.6mph, only 1mph slower than John Cobb's ultimate record of 143.44mph achieved in the Napier-Railton two months later.

George Eyston drove two streamlined MGs in the thirties, 'Magic Midget' and 'Magic Magnette'. The latter had two bodies, a conventional two-seater for road racing and the streamlined single-seater used to attack Class G records. The Magnette first appeared in 1934 and took many records including the flying mile at 128.69mph and 120.88 miles in the hour. It was later fitted with an all-enveloping body by Reid Railton, and in this form was driven by A T 'Goldie' Gardner who took many more records with the car, often driving it on the closed motorway at Jabbekke in Belgium.

Riley scored one of their greatest successes in the 1935 British Empire Trophy Race, with first, second and third places in the 80 lap, 240 mile event. The winner was Freddy Dixon, followed by Percy Maclure and Joseph Paul. One of the rarer cars of the thirties was the Squire, a complex, beautifully constructed and very expensive 1.5 litre sports car. Luis Fontes drove a specially prepared racing version with a single-seat body by Markham in 1935, but had little success. His best result was third in the October Mountain Handicap Race. Adrian Squire was only 25 and Fontes 21, both were killed in the 1939–45 war.

The final development of the racing Austin Seven was the twin-ohv single-seater by Murray Jamieson in 1936. The 744cc engine developed an amazing 116bhp at 8,500rpm, and was capable of over 120 mph. It took many class records and held both the Mountain and Campbell circuit class records until the end of Brooklands. Third place in the 1937 International Trophy Race was taken by the dance band leader Billy Cotton in his MG K3 Magnette. He was a regular and popular driver in the later thirties.

W M Couper drove a famous old Talbot which started life as a 105 team car in the 1934 Alpine Trial and was later fitted with a streamlined racing body and a 3.3 litre 110 engine. It was developed to produce over 150bhp and could lap Brooklands at just under 130 mph, yet was tractable enough to be driven home after the day's racing through the Bank Holiday traffic.

Two 'Bimotre' Alfa-Romeos were built in 1935 to the order of Scuderia Ferrari, but were unsuccessful in road racing due to excessive tyre wear. One was brought to Brooklands in 1937 by Austin Dobson and broke the Class B Mountain record on its first

Fuelling up, JCC 200 race 1938 *Brooklands Museum*

appearance. The car had two 2.9 litre straight-eight engines, the second mounted back-to-front behind the driver; a single gearbox was underneath the driver. It was a great favourite with the crowds and on one occasion when it was withdrawn at the last minute from a race a number of the fans demanded their money back. In 1938 the car was bought by the Hon. Peter Aitken who removed the rear engine and ran it as the Alfa-Aitken, finishing second in the 1939 Mountain Handicap race.

In 1937 the Campbell Circuit was opened to provide something closer to road racing conditions than the track had provided up to then. Some 2.5 miles per lap, it consisted of a road cutting across the centre of the course from the middle of the Railway Straight to the Fork where it crossed the Finishing Straight and ran parallel to it to the foot of the Test Hill where a hairpin bend brought it back through the Public Enclosure to the beginning of the Members' Banking. The 1938 International Trophy Race used the Campbell Circuit and was won by Maclure's Riley, second place was taken by another rising star, Raymond Mays, in an ERA, a car which was a serious attempt to produce a real rival car to the continental giants who were dominating international racing. Only four cars finished the race, marred by an accident which claimed the lives of two spectators, one of them Murray Jamieson, the designer of the twin-ohc Austin Seven.

In 1936 Mays had won his first race, the Mountain Championship, in an ERA R4B, which was probably the finest model of the marque. In 1938 the JCC 200 Mile Race returned to Brooklands after two years at Donnington. It was no longer a light car race, being open to all-comers, though the fact that it was held over the Campbell Circuit excluded the really large cars such as Cobb's Napier-Railton. The race featured Prince Bira of Thailand in his 2.9 litre Maserati and Staniland's Alfa-Romeo-engined Multi Union. A gaggle of ERAs was driven by, among others, Mays, Cotton and the winner, Johnny Wakefield.

John Rhodes Cobb had a long and distinguished career at Brooklands. He first raced there in 1925 driving a 1910 FIAT; most of his career was spent at the wheel of cars varying in size from large to enormous. These included the TT Vauxhall, a 10.5 litre Delage, the Leyland-Thomas, 'Babs' and his own creation, the Napier-Railton. This was designed originally to attack the world 24-hour record, and was built to the design of Reid Railton in the Thomson and Taylor sheds on the far side of the circuit from the paddock and clubhouse at Brooklands. The car was powered by a 23,970cc

John Cobb with his Napier Railton at Bonneville 1935/36 *National Motor Museum*

Napier Lion aero engine which developed 505bhp, and had a single-seat body made by Gurney Nutting.

Driving this car Cobb won the 1935 BRDC 500 Mile Race at 121.28mph, and in October that year he set the Outer Circuit lap record of 143.44 mph. This was never beaten and remains the ultimate lap speed recorded at Brooklands. Cobb won the Brooklands '500' again in 1937 at 136.07 mph, the fastest speed of any race at this distance until the 1949 Indianapolis '500'. The Napier-Railton is still in running order and is on display at Brooklands Museum. It is coaxed back into life several times a year and makes public demonstration runs along the old runway, it is deafening if close to it and still exudes power and potential performance today.

Cobb's next car was the 'Railton Mobil Special' with which he made three successful attempts on the world land speed record, 350.2mph at Bonneville in September 1938; 369.7mph, again at Bonneville, in August 1939; and, in a lightened version of the car, 394.194mph in September 1947. This is the fastest speed ever recorded by a British internal combustion-engined car. It was too large a car to race at Brooklands, but Cobb demonstrated it at the track. Like the Napier-Railton it was built at Brooklands by Thomson and Taylor and was a lightweight design (3½ tons), and

Cobb (in car) and Reid Railton with the Railton Mobil Special 1938
National Motor Museum

had two 1250hp Napier Lion Aero engines. It was the first such car
to have the driving position in the nose ahead of the engines.

The car was displayed for many years in Birmingham Museum
of Science & Industry, but when that closed the car was moved to
the Donnington, East Midlands museum where it is still on
display. Rumours at the time were that the car was coming back
to Brooklands, but undoubtedly the problem of raising the
finance was insuperable, if in fact it was offered.

At the same time as Cobb was building the Railton-Mobil
Special, another Brooklands regular, George Eyston, was also
building his contender. 'Thunderbolt' was far from being a
lightweight and turned the scales at over 7 tons. It had four
paired wheels at the front and two at the rear driven by two
1175hp Rolls-Royce 'R' engines. Eyston set a new record at
Bonneville in November 1937 of 312mph, raising it to 345.5mph
in August 1938 only to see Cobb take it from him a month later.
'Thunderbolt' survived a German bomb whilst in storage during
WWII and in 1946 went to New Zealand as part of a British
Exhibition. There it was all but destroyed in a fire, the remains
are now in Auckland Museum of Transport & Technology.

Lady drivers were seen in increasing numbers during the

thirties, causing little comment as they drove and serviced their cars dressed in trousers, at a time when if seen elsewhere they would have aroused comment. In the early years before 1914, lady drivers had included Ethel Locke King, Dorothy Levitt, Muriel Thompson, Christabel Ellis and Ivy Cummings. There had only been two ladies' races before 1914 and it was 1929 before they were allowed to compete with the men.

Probably the most versatile of the ladies was Gwenda Hawkes who in 1922 had ridden a 129cc Trump-JAP motor cycle for two twelve hour periods at an average of 44.65mph. She later broke records on Rudge motor cycles and Morgan three-wheelers and set the ladies' lap record in a single-seat Derby Miller at 135.95mph in 1935. Other well-known, and successful, lady drivers in the thirties included Kay Petre driving Wolseley Hornets, Bugattis and even the 10.5 litre Delage, which she lapped at 134.75mph in 1935. She is best remembered as a member of the successful Austin Seven team.

Doreen Evans, Margaret Allan and Ivy Schwedler drove MGs, Elsie 'Bill' Wisdom, Austins and Rileys, and Miss P McOstrich and Miss L Wright (the only reference I have found is as formal as that) drove a Talbot 90 in 1934–35.

Over the years a number of American cars, or their derivatives, ran at Brooklands, from the Stanley and White steamers before the first World War, through the Whitney-Straight Dusenberg of the thirties which is preserved in the Brooklands Museum, to the 1935 Graham-Paige. This car was based on the American Lammas-Graham car, much modified. One particular Graham-Paige has a place in the records. Its chassis date is uncertain, though it must be before 1935 as the company only made 6 cylinder cars from that year. The straight eight was driven by G L Baker who had bought the car for £50 in 1935 when it seemed quite elderly then. He rebuilt the engine and fitted a long-tailed two-seater body made for him by Harrington of Hove. It was quite successful, lapping at over 107mph in 1936. At the 1939 August Bank Holiday meeting Baker won the third August Outer Circuit Handicap at 99.46mph. This was to be the last race ever to be run at Brooklands, though no-one saw it like that when the track closed down at the outbreak of World War II.

References
Brooklands, a Pictorial History: G N Georgano, 1978
The History of Motor Racing: William Boddy, 1978
The History of Brooklands Motor Course: William Boddy, 1957

CHAPTER 9

The Brooklands Story IV

Loose Ends and Post-1945

Motor Cycling

Although overshadowed by car racing, motorcycle events were frequently held at Brooklands. The earliest recorded event was in February 1908 when two Oxford undergraduates held a private competition over one lap. The winner was W G McMinnies, later the editor of 'Motor Cycling', on a 3.5hp Triumph. The first official race took place at the 1908 Easter meeting when a two-lap scratch race was included among the car races. Twenty one riders took part, it was won by Will Cook on a 984cc Peugeot at 63mph.

Handicapping was introduced at the May 1908 meeting and the next year the British Motor Cycle Racing Club was formed. Sidecar racing began in 1911 and soon became popular. The BMCRC fifth meeting in 1912 took place on the 20th July, one of the successful riders was an Australian, Les Bailey, riding a 350cc Douglas flat twin machine. He won the five lap All Comers Handicap and also made the fastest climb of the day on the Test Hill (see the next section). At the summit Bailey left the ground for at least twelve feet, the first time such a phenomenon had been recorded.

One of the most remarkable motorcycles to appear at Brooklands was the Temple-Anzani in 1923. It was designed by Hubert Hagens for C F Temple and had an Anzani ohc V-twin engine in a double loop frame. It won a number of races and in November 1923 Temple raised the World Flying Start Kilometre record to 108.85mph, with a one-way run at 113.49mph. At the Whitsun 1924 event the Temple-Anzani, again ridden by Temple, won the fastest motorcycle race yet held at the track, at 105.52mph.

In the twenties the Auto Cycle Union Six Day Trial for motorcycles and three-wheelers included Brooklands at the end of the itinerary for a high-speed trial which always eliminated a number of competitors, coming as it did at the end of five tiring days on the road covering some 850 miles. The Motor Cycle Club

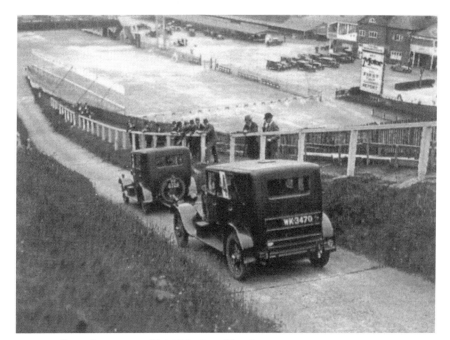

Descending the Test Hill 1929 *Brooklands Museum*

organised popular members' meetings for machines in touring trim. The fastest touring machine ever was Tisdall's BMW when, at the September 1938 One Hour High Speed Trial, it lapped at between 91 and 95mph. The breaking of the magic 100mph lap was eagerly awaited, alas it was never to be realised before the track closed in 1939.

The Test Hill
As well as racing, Brooklands was frequently used for testing cars and components, both by manufacturers and the motoring press. The Motor published a regular series in the thirties based on detailed performance tests of sporting and family cars on the track and on the 'Test Hill.' The hill was also used independently for a form of hill-climb events.

The Test Hill was, and remains, a severe test for any car or motorcycle. The last 50 yards is a 1 in 4 gradient. The all-time record for the hill was made in 1932 by 'The Terror' in 7.45 seconds. The car 'flew' 40 ft. at the top before landing.

The Social Scene
The Paddock and the Café were centres of activity and gossip and provided endless sources of interest to those who were

fanatical about cars and racing – and aeroplanes and flying too – but that is another story. It was the place to be, and to be seen, by the London 'smart set', and vied with Ascot and Henley on the social calendar in the thirties. Bookmakers were there from the beginning, remembering that much of the early organisation was based on horse-racing practices and procedures. They usually operated near to the Lap Scoring Board, but were also to be found in the Paddock.

Artists such as Gordon Crosby were regularly to be seen in the Paddock, his drawings featured in the Autocar for many years, and the originals fetch high prices today. It was Crosby who designed the famous BARC car badge in 1931.

It was the outbreak of the Second World War that finished Brooklands. The racing circuit and airfield were handed over to Vickers-Armstrongs and the track was breached in several places to construct aircraft research and manufacturing buildings. After the war most of the buildings continued in use by Vickers, and in any case the track had deteriorated so much that it was virtually beyond repair, added to which the increased speed and sophistication of post-war racing cars called for a different type of circuit. The quality of the concrete surface had never been high and the new low-slung racing cars would have found the track far too bumpy and rough if not outright dangerous.

Post 1945

No one thought in 1939 that the track would never open again as a sporting and social centre. When the sell-out of the site to Vickers after the war was announced there was disbelief and anger from those who had looked forward to the resumption of racing. But it was not to be. Most sporting motorists accepted the inevitable and moved their interests elsewhere. A faithful nucleus of devotees made annual pilgrimages to the site each summer, Vickers always being most co-operative. But the track was overgrown and hidden by trees which had been planted in 1939 as camouflage. Disused aircraft manufacturing materials were abandoned around the site on those parts of the concrete still visible. Part of the Clubhouse was used by Barnes Wallis as a design office, and a test-chamber had been built alongside, together with hangars.

William Boddy, then the editor of Motor Sport, wrote in February 1946: "A banked circuit that Mr. Locke King gave us at Brooklands enabled scientific testing to be carried out such as can never be undertaken over a road or artificial-road circuit. All manner of vehicles, of varying speeds, could be safely allowed on

Brooklands at the same time, and records of all kinds could be attempted there. Moreover the track was conveniently situated close to London."

Dame Ethel Locke King outlived her husband and just before she died in her ninetieth year in 1956 she wrote to Boddy: " Mr. Locke King made the Track with the intention of benefitting British engineers, sportsmen and motor designers and when, at first, it received little public support, he always said he believed its future was in the hands of the young. So for a while it proved to be and after his death I did all I could to allow their impetus full scope. But I was too old to carry on. It was open to the Trade, the Clubs and those who enjoyed Brooklands to buy the place, or to secure the direction of the Company when the purchasers offered shares to the public, but there was no support from any of these... I hope someone with Mr. Locke King's initiative will come to the front and make some other track, perhaps better suited to modern requirements."

On the sixtieth anniversary of the opening of the track, a small band formed The Brooklands Society, their object being to maintain contact with drivers, mechanics and officials from pre-war days. They met each June to reminisce about the old days and admire the pre-war cars they brought along. Membership grew rapidly and was extended to anyone with an interest in the track.

In 1973 a small group of volunteers started on the huge task of clearing the remaining track and bankings of the thirty year's growth of trees and bushes. After four year's work on Sundays they had cleared the remaining concrete track, banking and the Members' Hill. In 1975 the hill was used for the annual reunion meeting. The aim was to retain the remaining parts of the site and to establish a museum of motoring and flying. The remaining buildings were listed and when news came out that the historic site could be coming up for sale there was frenzied activity to ensure that developers did not destroy the site.

When Gallaghers made a successful bid for the land on which to build their new headquarters, planning consent was granted so long as the historic buildings and access to them was preserved. The company went far beyond their legal requirements and contributed to the rebuilding of a joint approach road and gave additional land to the Brooklands Trust which had by then been formed. The Trust has gone from strength to strength developing the museum each year. The small professional staff is supplemented by a large band of volunteers and by the 'Friends of Brooklands' which was formed in 1987.

In the twenty-first century plans have been announced for a further major development of parts of the other side of the site away from the museum across the Wey, including the remaining

The Members' banking today *Peter Tarplee collection*

The Clubhouse today *Peter Tarplee collection*

aircraft runway and areas beyond it towards existing temporary commercial development and the Byfleet banking. Mercedes (UK) Ltd. have, as this is being written, received planning consent to build a test and development centre, a museum and an hotel, as well as to restore part of the grass runway and to build a small test track. Also to landscape the remaining area – with public access – to include flood-prevention measures which should prevent a repetition of the disastrous floods which badly affected the museum in November 2000. Already work has begun on clearing the undergrowth from the remaining parts of the Byfleet banking. This development will bring a prestigious addition to enhance the museum and conserve the historic site and one hopes that it will succeed.

References

The History of Brooklands Motor Course: William Boddy, 1957
The History of Motor Racing: William Boddy, 1978
Brooklands, a Pictorial History: G N Georgano, 1978

Two Centenarian Manufacturers

There are two vehicle manufacturers in Surrey who have both completed one hundred years in production. These are Dennis and AC. Both have had their triumphs and near disasters, Dennis nearly failing at least twice during the second half of the twentieth century, and are again in difficulty as this book is being finalised. AC have had financial traumas on and off throughout their history, and have gone through one more just prior to this account being written. They are both stories of endeavour and the products and personalities behind them are worth telling in some detail.

Dennis of Guildford

The origins of the firm are strikingly similar to that of Morris in Oxford. John Dennis (1871–1939) served an apprenticeship with an ironmonger in his native Bideford in Devon. He came to Guildford where he took up a post with Filmer & Mason in the High Street. There he assembled and sold bicycles, later he worked in London for a supplier of bicycle parts, returning to Guildford in 1895 to open his own bicycle business, 'The Universal Athletic Stores', at 94 High Street, on the south side of the street close to the bridge.

Sales of his 'Speed King' & 'Speed Queen' cycles, which were assembled in the back garden, were assisted by cycling lessons given by his brother Raymond, later Sir Raymond (1878–1939), who had joined him after the new shop had opened. They developed the business into making their own bicycles and patented a pneumatic saddle and an improved frame design. They exhibited at the Crystal Palace in 1899 and the space behind the shop developed into a factory area. Examples of Dennis bicycles survive locally, one is in the Dennis factory museum, and another is owned by Les Bowerman of Ripley.

In July 1899 a motorised tricycle was built under the 'Speed King' name, it was powered by a 3.5 hp de Dion engine at the rear, and had tiller steering. John Dennis drove up Guildford

High St. in the car at 'a furious pace of 16 mph', for which he was duly convicted by the local magistrates. The Dennis brothers turned this into a triumphant advertisement for their vehicle.

Next came the 'Quadricycle', their first four-wheeled vehicle, which Raymond successfully raced, bringing in orders. The company records from 1901 to 1955, with incomplete records since then, are now preserved in the Surrey History Centre in Woking, but they do not always tell the whole story. For instance they do not record the reason why, in 1900, the brothers took out a lease on the old barracks building at the end of Friary St. It can only be because the demand for their vehicles had outstripped the capacity of the restricted premises at 94 High St. It can only be for the same reason that less than a year later the business moved into a purpose-built three-storey factory on the corner of Onslow St. and Bridge St. The first proper car was made in 1901 in the new factory. This car had an 8hp de Dion engine mounted at the front, a 3-speed gearbox with direct drive on top, and shaft drive.

The new building still stands, and is known as the Rodboro Building, after the Boot & Shoe company who took it over from Dennis in 1919. The architect was a local man, John Lake, and the contractor was Drowley & Co. of Woking. It has had a chequered career and was empty in the 1990s and becoming

The Rodboro building *Transbus Dennis*

near derelict until Guildford Borough Council took matters in hand and made it safe and waterproof as part of their riverside development plans. There were a number of proposals to renovate the building in the 1990s which did not materialise, demolition was threatened, which was stayed by a Grade II listing. One of the more appropriate adaptive re-use proposals was to convert the upper floors into offices for South East Arts with an industrial museum on the ground floor; this proposal was strongly supported by the Surrey Industrial History Group; others included a supermarket. Eventually the building was realistically adapted into a Wetherspoon pub. The pub contains many references to, and memorabilia of, Dennis; the owners and the architects, Tuffin, Ferraby & Taylor, received the SIHG conservation award in 2000.

The Rodboro Building is important, not only locally, but nationally and internationally, for it is considered to be the oldest extant purpose-built multi-storey car factory in the world. There is an older building in Coventry but it was converted from a textile mill and renamed The Motor Mills in 1895. It was occupied first by the Horseless Carriage Company and then by Daimler. It was badly bombed during WWII but the surviving buildings were used post-war by Coventry Climax to assemble fork lift trucks, today it is in multi-purpose use by several small businesses. A building which vied for the title with the Rodboro was the Renault factory on an island in the river Seine in Paris, but that was demolished in the late 1990s. Additional land was bought by the Dennis brothers in 1903, but only after opposition from within the Council. Two additions were made to the factory in 1903 and 1905. Although the surviving minute books do not state the reasons for the extensions, it was at this time that the decision was made to cease making bicycles and obviously additional capacity was required following the intention to concentrate on cars and commercial vehicles. Fire engines and buses soon followed.

The brothers always seemed to have the ability to identify the best market position for themselves, looking for what today we would call 'a niche market'. They withdrew from head-on competition with larger volume manufacturers, first of bicycles, and later of cars. In July 1901, 'Dennis Bros. Ltd.', a private company, was formed with four directors, seven subscribers and a capital of £7,500, increased to £100,000 in 1906. John Dennis was the first Chairman, the brothers alternating in this position until 1913.

1902 Dennis car, owned and still run by John Dennis *Transbus Dennis*

The 1902 catalogue issued by 'The Oldest Motor Makers in England' stressed that "the process of experiment in a firm which from the first held an unrivalled reputation for a perfect combination of scientific design and accurate workmanship placed them in the forefront of technical development and sales". Among the improvements listed for 1902 were "a new double-acting metal drum brake, a silencer and direct drive". Twelve distinguishing features of Dennis cars were quoted, among which were "no belts, no chains". Dennis were almost unique at the time in having direct, geared drive, when virtually everyone else still used belt or chain drive. The cars were advertised as "an 8-horse power model at 280 guineas, with a detachable awning for an extra 25 guineas". A 10hp model was 320 guineas and the Converted Quadricycle a mere 115 guineas. Tricycles were dropped at this time. The small de Dion-engined cars had soon been supplemented by 2 and 4-cylinder Aster-engined models of 12/14 and 16/20 hp. At least one 40hp 'Gordon Bennett' racing type was built with a Simms engine. In 1904 the famous patented overhead worm drive was introduced and continued until the end of car production.

The first commercial vehicle was produced in 1904, soon joined by charabancs and fire engines, the vehicle with which

1904 First commercial vehicle built, a 25cwt van sold to Harrods
Transbus Dennis

many people most associate the name of Dennis. The 1904
vehicle was a 25 cwt. van sold to Harrods and was fitted with a
two-cylinder de Dion engine and the patented worm final drive.
It featured a separate subframe carrying the engine,
transmission and auxiliaries to minimise the stress from torque.

The Onslow Street site soon became too small and
overcrowded and was first extended in 1903. The same year as
the second extension was built, 1905, a 31 acre site on
Woodbridge Hill was bought and the first workshop there, a
large redundant mission hall, was moved from Brixton and
erected. This survived until 1985. Ten additional workshops
were erected between 1910 and 1936, and a generating station in
1915. The Onslow Street site remained in use as offices and for
servicing cars from 1911 to 1919 when it was sold.

In 1906 larger 30/35hp engines were used in the cars, these
were made by White and Poppe, and soon afterwards Dennis
standardised on this engine supplier, some being made specially
to Dennis requirements. A wide range of reliable touring cars
were built, from 15.9 to 60hp, the latter being a short-lived
model built only between 1910 and 1911. In 1906 a Dennis car
performed so well in a 4,000 mile reliability trial that the next
year the company was awarded the Dewar Trophy in recognition

1908 First fire engine, built for City of Bradford Fire Dept. *Transbus Dennis*

of their achievement. By 1907 the commercial vehicle range comprised 15 & 30 cwt., 2, 3, 4 & 5-ton models, the latter being one of the largest on the market. Many of these used the Coventry-built White & Poppe four-cylinder T-head 40 hp engine.

The first fire engine was built in 1908 for the City of Bradford Fire Dept. In 1913 the decision was made to cease car production, the last models being 15.9 and 24hp four-cylinder models. A new 3.5 ton lorry was introduced, becoming one of the War Department 3 ton subvention models in 1914. Over 7,000 were built during WWI. Meanwhile in 1913, Dennis Bros. (1913) Ltd. was floated as a public company with £300,000 share capital. George Clare, who had supervised the setting up of the new company, and Reginald Downing joined the board. Clare became the first Chairman, with the Dennis brothers as joint Managing Directors. The flotation was brought about by the first of a number of financial crises the business has gone through.

John was the technical 'ideas' man at the factory, whilst Raymond in the twenties and thirties travelled the world as a very effective salesman. More in the public eye than his brother he was knighted in 1920 following a world tour. He said at the time that the honour should have gone to John, for without his technical abilities there would have been no product for

Raymond to sell. Downing had worked for the Dennis brothers since 1902 as a draughtsman and trials driver with a particular interest in fire engines.

In 1918 the company reverted to its original name of Dennis Bros. Ltd., and several new developments took place. During the war virtually all production had been given over to building the 3 ton subvention lorry, orders for which ceased when the war finished. John put in hand several diversification projects, in 1920 into lawn-mowers, and then in 1921 into refuse vehicles. In 1919 a new engine design was wanted and John instigated a merger with White & Poppe, who had been their main engine supplier since 1909. Production was rationalised between the two factories; engines, clutches and gear boxes all being made in the Coventry factory.

A subsidiary company, Dennis Portland, was floated to market the new 2–2.5 ton commercial chassis. By 1920 the company had agents in Bombay, Singapore, Batavia, Hong Kong, Tokyo, Sydney, Wellington, Honolulu, Valparaiso, Buenos Aires and New York. Dennis Contracts was formed to operate a hire-purchase scheme. 2,000 heavy chassis were made in 1923, this level of production was maintained most years until the depression in the early thirties. In 1925 a new 30 cwt. model was introduced with either normal or forward control, proving very popular. In 1927 further forward control models were introduced including the 'M' type 12 ton six-wheeler which was not a success. It seems to have been underpowered and not competitively priced.

Bus chassis were becoming important during the twenties, both the London General Omnibus and Aldershot & District companies being almost totally Dennis equipped. In 1928 the first 'H' Type double-decker, with a fully enclosed top deck, appeared with a 5.7 litre engine. Many were fitted with a 52 seat aluminium body made by Shorts of Rochester, who diversified into bus bodies when aircraft orders fell away. Aldershot & District bus bodies were generally made by Hall & Lewis.

Between 1930 and 1932 850 'GL' Light Duty buses were built. Brush built many of the bodies and the model seated 14–16 passengers. The 'Lancet' fire engine, normal or forward control, and based on the same chassis as a bus, was popular in the early thirties. One was shown at Buenos Aires in March 1931 and a large order for bonneted versions was obtained.

During the thirties several important events took place. The firm introduced a diesel engine into its product line for the first

Guildford fire engine and the fire station in North Street in the twenties
Transbus Dennis

Dennis production line in the thirties *Transbus Dennis*

time and the same year, 1932, a major extension to No. 9 shop
was authorised. Into this was moved the entire engine
manufacturing of White & Poppe, that company ceasing to exist

Ace fire engine 1935 *Transbus Dennis*

from that time. To accommodate the new work force, many of whom had moved down from Coventry, 102 houses were built to the west of the factory. 'Dennisville' was in addition to the 121 houses already owned by the company. There were no fewer than seven patent applications in 1932, and increasing output during the thirties was sold through an ever growing number of foreign outlets. Several Royal Warrants were awarded during this time.

In 1932 Surbiton Urban District Council ordered one of the new 250–400 gallons per minute motor pumps, with hose reel equipment and a 35 foot extension ladder. It had chromed finished metal parts, rather than the usual brass, and was the first of many such appliances to be ordered by British local authorities. One of the undoubted successes of the thirties was the 40/45 cwt. 'Ace' chassis of 1935, which had the engine ahead of the front axle resulting in the nickname of 'flying pig'. It was fitted with a variety of lorry body styles, bus, coach and fire engine bodies, and several types of refuse and gully emptier bodies. It competed successfully with competition from the mass production suppliers. The 'Big Four' and 'Light Six' chassis of 1935 were popular with fire brigades and were usually fitted with an extension ladder and large capacity water tank. In 1937 the 'Max' 12 ton six-wheel chassis and a 5 ton four-wheeler were introduced.

War time Churchill tank production *Chris Shepheard collection*

Post-war bus body construction *Transbus Dennis*

In 1939 both Dennis brothers died 'in harness' within a few months of each other, thus severing the family connection. Some

101

Air view of Woodbridge Hill factory *Transbus Dennis*

2,000 were by then employed in the business. The brothers were fine examples of spectacular engineering and commercial success. John's son, Royston, had joined the board in 1929 and became Assistant to the Managing Director in 1933. He had resigned in 1938 and went to live in S. Africa. He joined the RAOC during WWII attaining the rank of major. Raymond seemingly never married, he had no children anyhow.

During WWII all production was for the war effort, consisting of lorries – some 3,000 WD 'Max' 6/8 tonners were built – agricultural vehicles, bombs, Churchill tanks, fire pumps and infantry carriers. With 24 hour working the labour force was doubled to 4,000. After the war there was an insatiable demand for vehicles of all kinds and 1946–1951 were the best years for the company, with improvements in bus design, a new refuse collection vehicle and a new series of fire engines.

I have seen it stated that Dennis never built their own bus or coach bodies, but in fact prior to, and immediately after WWII, the firm built wooden-framed coach and bus bodies as well as commercial vehicle and ambulance bodies in-house.

Lightweight 'Stork' & 'Heron' trucks were built in the 1950s as well as the very successful 'Pax' with an ohv 6-cylinder 80 bhp petrol engine developed from the pre-war 5 tonner. The 'Lance' double-decker bus was introduced in 1950 and a large fleet was

Coach for Aldershot & District Co. *Transbus Dennis*

supplied to the Aldershot & District bus company. The 'Lancet' single deck bus was introduced in 1951 and in 1953 the Aldershot & District ordered a 'one-off' underfloor 'Lancet'. The successor to the 'Lance' was the 1958–1960 'Lo-line', a version of the successful Bristol 'Lodekka', again Aldershot & District were major buyers.

The 22 ton 'Pax' V truck with a Perkins diesel engine in the mid 1960's was developed into the less successful 'Maxi' 30 ton tractor in 1968. The 'Paxit' refuse vehicle was introduced in the 1960's fitted with compression and ram-ejection equipment. In 1962 the Fire Appliance Section of Alfred Miles was acquired and in 1964 so was the Mercury Truck & Tractor Co., who specialised in airfield vehicles.

A programme of modernisation was undertaken in 1965 but there was a large trading loss at the end of the year, productivity being inferior to that of major competitors. Recovery was assisted in 1968 by a huge contract to re-equip the entire frontline fire appliance fleet for the London Fire Brigade. A potential merger with Seddon came to nothing in 1969. A further re-organisation of the company and the production facilities from 1969 to 1972 did not succeed in keeping the business profitable, in spite of a virtually full order book, but in 1969 the successful DB 15.5 ton tipper truck had an edge over other 16 ton gross competitors by saving on excise duty.

In 1972 the company was taken over by the Hestair Group and renamed Dennis Motors Ltd, and the next year, Hestair Dennis. The Mercury and Miles businesses were sold off as was the

170 seat double decker for Hong Kong *Transbus Dennis*

mower diversification, the latter with the right to use the Dennis name – to Qualcast – and is now called the Dennis Derby. The refuse vehicle business was transferred to Hestair's own company in Warwick, where they continued to be produced under the Dennis badge. Dennis commercial vehicle production was reduced to a single model, the 'Delta', with a 16 ton payload and either a Gardner or Perkins diesel engine. It had an Ogle-designed steel tilt cab with aluminium and fibre glass panels for lightness. Some 40 six-wheeled 'Condor' and 'Dragon' long wheelbase double-decked buses had been built for the Kowloon Motor Bus Co. and the Kai Tak Motor Bus Co. in Hong Kong by 1984, repeat orders have followed on since then. The buses can seat 170 passengers, have bodies by Duple and engines by Gardner.

In 1984 the business was again in financial difficulties and was sold to Trinity Holdings, who re-named the company Dennis Specialist Vehicles. In 1985 there was a massive re-organisation involving redundancies and the selling off of most of the Woodbridge site for re-development, including the scheduled facade alongside the railway line. A popular coach design of the mid 1980s was the 'Lancet' Highline midi-coach with a 150hp Perkins engine and a German ZF gearbox. Bodies were fitted by several suppliers, the 'Alize' by Van Hool of Belgium being particularly favoured by customers including the local firm of

104

Air view of Slyfield estate factory *Transbus Dennis*

Bicknell. Fire engines at this time were on the 'Rapier' and 'Sabre' chassis.

There was a successful management buyout in 1989, the Woodbridge site being completely closed down in 1990 and the business moved to a new purpose-built factory on the Slyfield estate in Guildford. Commercial vehicle production ceased at the same time, the firm now concentrating solely on fire engine and bus & coach chassis, the 'Lancet' coach and 'Sabre' fire engine chassis remaining the mainstay of production.

In 1998 the business changed hands once again, amid speculation in the financial press that it was to be closed down. There was a very public tussle between Mayflower and Henlys for control. But the eventual new owners, Mayflower, who owned the Alexander body-building firm in Scotland, pushed ahead with development of new models, and standardised on Cummins engines, US designed but built in Britain. There was yet another management change in 2000 when the two protagonists, Mayflower and Henlys, decided to sink their differences and merge the Dennis and Alexander businesses of Mayflower with the Plaxton body-building part of Henlys, to create Transbus International. The new company was 70% owned by Mayflower and 30% by Henlys. The Chairman was John Fleming, a joint Managing Director of Mayflower. The deal was based on the relative size of the two companies' bus businesses.

By 2003 Transbus International had 35–40% of the British bus building market and sales of £460m. It meant that orders came to Guildford with bodies subsequently built by whichever of the coachbuilders in the Group is specified by the customer. There of course is other business to be won from customers who will have their bodies built by firms such as the Belgian company Van Hool. Overseas orders continue, the Far East being a particularly strong market. Bodies are fitted locally in both Singapore and Hong Kong. Further orders were received recently for the 170-seat, three-axled double-decker buses. The market for fire engines continues, although there is strong competition for both home and export orders from Mercedes and MAN in Germany, and Volvo and Scania in Sweden. There was much local criticism when Surrey County Council re-equipped in the 1990s largely with Volvo fire engines rather than support the local business, but Dennis did gain some orders. Again the Far East is still a good market, customers preferring to place repeat orders with a supplier they know and trust.

Models in production by Transbus Dennis in early 2004 are 'Sabre' fire engines with all steel tilt cabs, Cummins 'C' series engines of up to 250 bhp and Allison automatic transmissions

Dart midi-bus 2004 *Transbus Dennis*

and gearboxes. The 'Javelin' is a high payload, low weight coach chassis with either a 240 or 290bhp turbo-charged Cummins engine and ZF powered steering and 6-speed gearbox. The 'Lance' is a low-floor design allowing for easy disabled wheelchair access and has similar technical specifications to the 'Javelin'. The 'Dart' midi bus is the most common bus on British roads today and is built in a range of versions, 8.5m, 9m & 9.5 m long with a range of body width options, giving seating for up to 60 passengers.

Bus and coach chassis are welded structures but those for fire engines are still of bolted construction. Assembly of the engines, transmissions, power steering, pumps etc., onto the chassis are carried out in the factory with units and components from suppliers world-wide. Engines from Cummins, ZF steering units and gearboxes from Germany, Allison transmissions from the US and other components from Sweden, Spain and elsewhere. The chassis are today tested on a rolling road within the factory, no longer do we see body-less vehicles out in all weathers clocking up test mileage on the roads around Guildford.

There is no fire engine body builder in the present group structure, but approved builders include Carmichael of Worcester, Merryweather of London and John Dennis Coachbuilders who are also on the Slyfield estate. John is the son of Royston, and thus the grandson of the first John. He set up his own business in Merrow repairing fire engine bodies, moving to

Rescue vehicle for Surrey Fire Service *Transbus Dennis*

the Slyfield estate in 1991 where new fire engine bodies are now built as well as continuing with repairs. It is a completely separate firm from Transbus Dennis, John has retained an interest in the firm carrying his name since he sold the business in 2001. John Dennis owns three early Dennis cars, from 1902, 1909 and 1915, the latter built on a light commercial chassis. All are roadworthy and have run from time to time on the Brighton Anniversary Run held in November each year. There is a small museum inside the Transbus Dennis Works containing one of John Dennis' cars, a bicycle, 1914 and 1936 fire engines and a lawn-mower.

Unfortunately in late March 2004 it was revealed that a £20m 'black hole' had been discovered in the accounts of Transbus International and that it had £180m of debt. Fleming and other directors resigned and the group was placed in the hands of administrators Deloitte & Touche. The future must be bleak unless new owners can be quickly found. A contributory factor to the situation was alleged to be the excessive price paid, and subsequent high debt incurred, when taking over Dennis.

Many of the extensive archives of the company have fortunately been preserved and are held in the Surrey History Centre in Woking. The ethos of the firm has remained throughout; no long production runs and each order made to the customer's individual requirements but of course using standardised components as much as possible. Components would be produced in advance in the early days but little attempt was made to influence customers. Minute books and annual reports record the value of advance orders, but it is clear that – except in wartime – no production line in the accepted sense existed. Each vehicle, as the works production orders make clear, had its own individual features as specified by the customer. Today, chassis are fabricated on site and then assembled with a range of components from many parts of the world. In the Rodboro factory it was the opposite. Virtually every component was made on site, only by so doing did the brothers feel that they could ensure that the high standard they laid down was maintained.

It is unfortunate, but true I am sure, that though the engineering ingenuity and high quality of the product always was, and still is, the hallmark of Dennis vehicles, during the fifties to the eighties this was gradually working to their detriment in a world where in-built obsolescence seemed to be becoming the norm. Today once again the company is concentrating on specialised products and markets, and have been holding their own in a very competitive international market place.

An examination of the range of patents taken out by the British motor industry over the years shows the true place of Dennis Bros. in history. The first, and much publicised patent in 1904 for worm drive and gearing, was claimed to ensure a virtually silent, long lasting and smooth transmission. Many other patents followed over the years, mostly in the name of John Dennis.

The future of the business is hopefully secure and one trusts that it may long continue.

AC Cars of Thames Ditton

In 1900 John Weller, then in his early twenties, designed a 20hp car which he put into production under his own name in West Norwood, London in 1903 and exhibited at the Crystal Palace the same year. The *Autocar* wrote at the time "... in all the details of the Weller car, there is food for much reflection. We foresee a brilliant future for the Weller car and its talented designer." John Portwine, a successful butcher and the owner of a number of shops in South London, backed Weller financially. Production difficulties arose and with costs mounting it was decided to move into the cheaper end of the car market. Portwine suggested something for the commercial market and thus was born the three-wheeled 'Autocarrier' with a 5.6 hp air-cooled single cylinder engine with chain drive to the single rear wheel. The vehicle found a ready market, customers included the Great Western and London & South Western Railways, The Army & Navy Stores, Selfridges and the United Yeast Co. who had a fleet of over 70 Autocarriers.

In 1907 Weller turned to manufacturing a passenger version of the Autocarrier and set up a new company, 'Autocars and Accessories Ltd.', with Weller and Portwine as directors. He produced the AC 'Tricar' based on the commercial vehicle with the passenger seated in the front and the driver behind and above the single cylinder engine and in front of the single rear wheel. Steering was by a tiller and the car weighed only 4.5 cwt. ready for the road. This was the first use of the abbreviation 'AC' which has remained in use ever since. In 1907 the two seat vehicle sold for £85 and was replaced the next year by the 'Sociable' with the driver and passenger side-by-side, this version selling for £95. Demand outstripped the capacity at West

1908 AC Sociable *Peter Tarplee collection*

AC Ferry Works, Thames Ditton *Peter Tarplee collection*

Norwood and the factory moved to the Ferry Works at Thames Ditton. This factory had been built by Willans & Robinson in 1880 to manufacture high speed steam engines for yachts and launches. In 1886 most of the factory was accidentally burned down. It was quickly rebuilt and was back in full production by the end of 1889. The factory was mostly all on one level, only the offices, the pattern shop and the 'mess rooms' being housed in a three-storey building. By 1890 the works was too small and over the next three years the firm moved to a new factory in Rugby where it was eventually to become part of English Electric and subsequently GEC.

Weller now reformed the company at Thames Ditton and registered it as 'Autocarriers (1911) Ltd.' and continued to expand output of the three-wheeler, which stayed in production until 1914. The first four-wheeled car at Thames Ditton came out in 1913. This was a 10hp light car with a three-speed gearbox integral with the rear axle; the engine was a 1,100cc French Fivet. The new four-wheeler did not go into full production until 1918, the factory making shells and fuses during the war. Additional buildings had been erected during the war in the High Street and stood the firm in good stead later on. Weller sought to build the lightest car he could consistent with safety and road-holding and was an early advocate and user of aluminium in the combined gearbox and back axle. He could not find an engine which met his requirements in England so bought the Fivet which powered all the four-wheeled cars up to 1914.

In 1913 the car was tested on the track at Brooklands, the first instance of a long connection between AC and the circuit. It lapped at 35mph and reached 45mph on the Railway Straight, a not insignificant speed for a light car of the period. In 1918 production restarted but the French engines were no longer available as the factory had been destroyed during the war. Some engine castings were found and brought to Ditton where they were completed. Then Weller arranged for the Anzani engine company to produce an engine to his design until it could be made at Ditton. It was 1925 before this was achieved. The engine was a 4 cylinder 11.8 hp under the old RAC system. Post war the car was fitted with a disc transmission brake and electric lights. The 4 cylinder car was to remain in production under constant development until 1928.

In 1919 Weller produced his famous single ohc 'light-six' engine. It was rated at 15.7 hp (1991 cc) and weighed under 350 lbs. It had an iron cylinder head, a steel flywheel and aluminium engine case and sump. The overhead camshaft engine was the first to be driven by a vertical shaft using helical gears. Weller introduced a system of endless chains to drive the camshaft and patented a spring plate tensioner coupled to an inverted driving chain. The car was fitted with a disc transmission brake and an

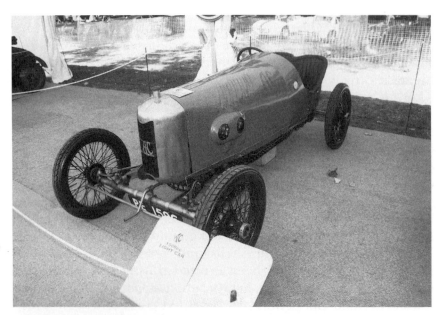

1918 AC 1500cc racer *Gordon Knowles collection*

1921 AC with 11.9hp Anzani engine *National Motor Museum*

integral rear-axle gearbox. This engine stayed under continuous development, and in production, until 1963. In 1920 '1911' was dropped from the firm's title, it becoming 'Autocarriers Limited.' In 1921 4-cylinder production was increased to meet demand and the car was to be seen at rallies throughout the country, often winning the 'Concours d'Elegance' award as well as best times for its class.

Selwyn F Edge joined the board in 1921 and in September 1922 became Chairman when both Weller and Portwine resigned in circumstances which were never completely made public, but were certainly connected with the financial difficulty in which the business was found to be. This was unfortunately not to be the only time. Weller continued as 'design consultant', but withdrew his money from the business. Edge was a flamboyant and difficult figure determined to put 'his' company well on the map by turning to racing and the setting of endurance records. He was an Australian who had worked with Napier at Acton during the war. He had raced and broken records himself and once held the Gordon Bennett Trophy, the Blue Riband of International motor racing, setting the record in 1907 for the one-man 24 hour drive at an average of 65.6 mph. It is probably at this time that the slogan 'Amazing Cars' appeared on the outside of the gable wall of the factory at Thames Ditton. It outlived the company on the site and was still to be seen many years later, often puzzling the uninitiated.

The company name was again changed, this time to 'AC Cars Ltd.', Autocarrier was by now meaningless as none had been built since the war. The 4 cylinder 'light car' broke 57 track records at Brooklands during 1921. In April 1922 it took the 12 hours record at 68.52 mph, and in May took the 24 hour, actually 2 x 12 hours as night racing was not allowed, covering 1,709 miles at an average speed of 71.23 mph. In October 1923 the car took the Light Car Class record over 300 miles at 82.73 mph. The engine in the record breaking car was a special 4 cylinder ohv engine with 4 valves per cylinder.

Harry Hawker bought a racing chassis and engine, fitted it with a streamlined body designed by Weller and built by Sopwith at Kingston, and entered it in races at Brooklands. In 1921 he set new world records in the 1500 cc class, the flying half mile at 105.14 mph and the standing half mile at 61.43 mph. On 24 November 1922 J A Joyce drove the car at over 100 miles in the hour, the first man to do so. Hawker had lost his life in a flying accident three weeks after breaking the records in 1921. The Weller-Hawker car was remarkably successful, breaking records from 1500 cc to 2200 cc with 8, 12, 16 and 24 valve cylinder heads. S C H 'Sammy' Davis of the *Autocar* was another famous driver of the Thames Ditton cars, he too took many records including several long distance ones. During 1922, 44 awards were won, in 1923, 31, and in 1924, 46.

In 1925 Tom Gillett, of Bookham and the Blackburne engine company (see Appendix II) created a new record for the one-man 24-hour drive averaging 82.5 mph for 24 hours on the Montlhéry track outside Paris. Edge's record had stood for 17 years. Also in 1925 an AC was the first British car to be entered in the Monte Carlo Rally, driven by the Hon. Victor Bruce. In 1926 the car was entered again coming in first. Bruce and his co-driver Brunell were the first British winners of the Monte Carlo rally. A number of endurance and long distance reliability events were entered and successfully completed on numerous occasions, including in 1927 a 5,000 mile trip in Europe and North Africa, the car driven by the Bruces, husband and wife. The next year they drove to Petsamo in Finland, the furthest north that any mechanical vehicle had yet travelled.

In 1927 Edge introduced a new range of cars, given type names for the first time. The 'Acedes' was 2 seat drophead coupé, a lighter version being called the 'Aceca.' The external appearance of the cars was changed at this time, the bulbous radiator, reminiscent of a Morris Cowley, was replaced by a higher tapered design. Prices varied from £350 for the 'Royal' open 2/3 seater to £585 for a coachbuilt saloon on a lengthened chassis. These cars were fitted with the Weller designed six cylinder engine improved to now give 56 bhp compared to the original 40. The disc transmission brake and rear-axle gearbox

1927 AC Acedes Light Six *Peter Tarplee collection*

were also replaced by more traditional four-wheel brakes and a gearbox in the normal position behind the engine.

Also in 1927 Edge restructured the company financially and once again the name was changed, this time to 'AC (Acedes) Cars Ltd.', with Edge still as Managing Director and very much still in control. This was the period of the great depression and specialist car manufacturers like AC found the going tough. So much so that by 1929 the business was insolvent and went into voluntary liquidation. Edge left the company and took no further part in the car trade until his death in 1940.

The company was reformed in 1930 when the Hurlock brothers purchased the assets, 'W A E' becoming Managing Director and 'C F' General Manager. The Hurlocks were successful car dealers from Denmark Hill in South London who had been looking for somewhere to expand their interests. Their family story is worth telling in itself, but is not part of the Surrey motoring one. Ferry Works was disposed off and the business concentrated at High Street, Thames Ditton. Production of new cars was at a standstill but servicing facilities were continued for existing customers.

Production was re-started in 1931 with the AC 'Magna', a larger car than previous models, available as a three-seat coupé or a five seat saloon. It reverted to the rear axle gearbox design, or Three Star Axle as it was known at the factory. The car had redesigned springing with half-elliptic suspension at the front and hydraulic brakes. Subsequently a smaller and lighter version was produced, the 'Light Magna'. In the same year a brand-new design was begun with a gearbox in unit with the engine. The prototype did so well in the 1932 Scottish Motor Rally that the Hurlocks decided to do away with the rear-axle gearbox entirely and concentrate on the new design. So a new chassis was designed and the faithful Weller six cylinder engine refined still further. In 1933 the all new two litre 'Ace' was introduced, with either a four seat sportsman saloon or two seat drophead coupé body. The motoring press gave the car good reports. 'The *Autocar*' said, "The engine is one of the cleanest jobs ever designed ... Among cars of its class, it would be difficult to find one with more distinguished and attractive looks. It is a car which looks and feels right – a dignified car for everyday use combined with a sports car performance".

In March 1933 all the four cars entered in the RAC Hastings Rally won awards, taking 1st, 4th, 6th and 7th places. Mrs. Daniell who had come 7th then took the Concours d'Elegance prize. For 1934 the chassis was improved further and four models were offered, a 2-seat drophead coupé, a 4-seat coupé, a 4-seat sports tourer and a 4-seat saloon. The company advertising slogan was 'Thames Ditton, the Savile Row of Motordom'. Customer requirements were catered for, with variations in trim or body styling modifications. A four speed 'crash' gearbox was fitted at first but an all-syncromesh box was offered as an option in 1935, not always apparently to the liking of the more sporty owner who preferred the gate change box, even though – or perhaps because – it called for greater skill in operation. In 1934 the 2-door 'Greyhound' saloon was added to the range, it met with immediate success as a closed sports car.

Prices at this time varied from £435 to £450, whilst cars with special coachwork designed by the Earl of March cost £475 for the open version and £495 for the saloon. The radiator design was changed once again in 1935 to a flat version to take advantage of the new flat radiator core which was now readily available, being both cheaper and more efficient. Next the 'Aero Saloon' was introduced and a better design of folding hood for the coupés, improving speed, visibility when reversing and appearance. Another change for 1935 was the adoption of three SU carburetors as standard but the policy of leaving well alone was otherwise continued. Road tests confirmed a timed speed over a quarter mile at 80 mph and acceleration through the gears from 0 to 50 mph in under 15 seconds, quite impressive figures for the time.

The market was very competitive and prices were held down to £470 for the 2-seat Drophead and the 'Greyhound' saloon and to £500 for the 'Aero' saloon and £510 for the 'Family' saloon. The Family saloon was the first break away from sporting cars, an attempt to attract the 'family man' who wanted superior performance than that offered by the mass producers. Rally success continued, often Charles Hurlock competed himself. 1936 saw the introduction of a short-chassis sports car fitted with the 16/70 engine giving it a top speed of 90 mph. It had a 20 gallon fuel tank and a chrome slatted radiator grille.

In 1937 Wilson pre-selector gearboxes were offered as optional across the range, and automatic chassis lubrication was introduced. Sales started to the US and new body colours were added for this market. A brilliant scarlet was popular in the US but was thought to be 'too garish' for the home market. In 1938 a 'Competition Sports' was offered as well as the 2-seat drophead and 4-seat saloon.

By 1939 it was realised that the 'Ace' chassis could not be improved further so a new design was put in hand. This gave more space, particularly in the luggage compartment due to the underslung chassis being replaced with an overswept type. Longer front and rear springs were added as there had been some criticism that the earlier ones were 'a little harsh'. At the

1939 AC 16/80 *Gordon Knowles collection*

Engine bay of 1939 16/80 *Gordon Knowles collection*

117

same time the faithful Weller light-six engine was further developed by producing a 'Sports' engine with higher compression giving almost 90 brake horse power when fitted with an Arnott low pressure super-charger. The only indication externally of the super-charger was a small 'blister' on the bonnet line. The super-charged car gave 18 mpg, which was considered excellent considering the performance it gave.

During 1938 and 1939, before war was declared, the company undertook several government contracts for aircraft parts and for a four-wheeled trailer fitted with a water purification tank which was produced in large numbers. Further trailers were subsequently made for the fire-service, fitted with Ford V-8 engines and either a Sulzer or Tangye water pump. These were superseded by mounting the units on Ford or Bedford lorry chassis, the cabs and bodies for which were designed and built at Thames Ditton. During WWII all car production ceased and the whole factory was turned over to the production of water tank trailers, fire pump trailers and cab and body units. Aircraft parts contracts were stepped up when the company became linked to the Fairey Aircraft Co. producing flaps and other parts for 'Albacore' and 'Firefly' aircraft.

When the water tank contracts were fulfilled orders were placed for undercarriage units for the 'Hamilcar' tank-carrying glider. To increase factory space large premises were acquired at Taggs Island on the Thames upstream of Hampton Court. This factory produced gun sights and then thousands of complete six-pounder guns. Large numbers were also refurbished after service. The Pettard spigot mortar, flame throwers and a six battery rocket launcher were among the more unusual wartime products from Taggs Island. At the end of the war a special very secret radar van was being constructed together with a trailer to house the generator equipment.

Car production did not get under way immediately after the end of the war, as there were several government contracts still to complete. The Design Department however was free to start work on a new chassis which would again feature an underslung chassis at the rear to maintain the company reputation for road-holding. The Weller 6-cylinder engine now producing 74 bhp was once again refined to incorporate bronze bearing shells with white-metal liners, and a new water circulation system and more powerful Girling brakes were fitted, hydraulic at the front and mechanical at the rear. A prototype 4-seat drophead coupe was built in 1946, using a body shell still in stock from pre-war. A 2-

door saloon was developed and the first production models rolled out in October 1947. The bodywork was all enveloping and the car was 5' 7" wide across the front wings, the widest yet of any AC car. 1948 saw a massive export drive, part of that conducted by the whole of the British car industry. Minor modifications were made to the chassis and engine over the next few years but all efforts were in producing as many cars as possible to meet the huge post-war demand. Open sports car bodies were not made at the factory but by the Buckland Body Works in Hertfordshire, the cars marketed as the 'AC Buckland'.

Then came about a remarkable shift in design, almost reminiscent of Weller's original 'Autocarrier'. The Ministry of Works approached the company to design and build an 'All Weather Invalid Carriage'. The logic behind this government approach appears to have been based on wartime contacts and trust in the company's ability to design and produce a new model quickly. This simple, and rather crude, single-seat three-wheeler was built at Taggs Island from parts made at Thames Ditton. Over 3,000 were produced at a rate of some 50 per week, all fitted with a BSA 250 cc two-stroke motor cycle engine. The last was completed in 1976. One other oddity was the design and building of four electric trains for Southend Corporation to run on Southend pier.

1950 All Weather Invalid Carriage *Peter Tarplee collection*

The Hurlocks showed little interest in sporting activities at this time but some success in racing took place, notably in 1952 at Silverstone where Jim Mayers drove a race-prepared, but otherwise standard, 2-litre saloon, against factory prepared sports racing cars by Bristol, Riley and Sunbeam-Talbot. Tony Crook in a Bristol was unchallenged in front but Mayers eventually overcame the rest of the opposition to finish second in the 1500–2000cc class in the 16 lap Touring Car Race.

Another unusual product in the fifties was a prototype 150hp diesel-powered railcar for British Rail. Five were built by 1958 and ran successfully on trials in Scotland and the west country but no additional orders were forthcoming. Also following production of the invalid three-wheeler a commercial two-seater was developed powered in 1953 by a 350cc Villiers two-stroke engine, the Mk. 2 version of 1955 being fitted with reverse gearing. 1,500 examples of the 'Petite' were built. They were easy to drive and reliable and found a ready market in the petrol-starved situation following the Suez crisis, but did not have a long-term future and in spite of costing under £400 were dropped in 1958.

By 1952 it was obvious that AC needed a replacement for the 2-litre. The faithful Weller light-six engine could not be developed further and Z T Marczewski, an emigré Polish engineer who had joined the company in 1945 after service in

1954 Ace (left) and 1939 16/80 *SIHG collection*

1955 Aceca GT coupe *Peter Tarplee collection*

the RAF, undertook the design of a new engine. Progress was slow, a prototype air-cooled flat twin was followed by a flat-four in 1955 and then a straight six in 2.2, 2.4 and 2.8 litre form. It was evident that it would take a long time to develop one of these engines and even longer a car to put it in, and time was not on the side of the company. A car that could be put quickly into production was needed. Ernie Bailey of Buckland Bodies had seen a simply constructed sports car built by John Tojeiro which used as many standard commercial parts as possible, including surplus Lea-Francis engines. Tojeiro was invited to Thames Ditton where all agreed that his rather stark car could be 'civilised' with a windscreen, comfortable seating etc. and would take the AC engine. This car was hurriedly built, finished to the usual high AC standards, and displayed, without any fanfare, at the Earls Court show in 1954. The prototype AC 'Ace' was born, recalling the famous model of the same name from the thirties.

Back at the factory, Alan Turner and Desmond Stratton turned the car into a serious production model, and the completed article was immaculately turned out. It received rapturous reports in the motoring press. The *Autosport* road test said "About 10.5 secs. is occupied from going from a standstill to 60 mph ... the engine was dead smooth all the way up to 5,000rpm ... a full 80mph was available in third and it just topped 100mph in top".

121

1957 Ace-Bristol at Modena, 2004 *Peter Tarplee collection*

In the first year some 60 cars were built, over half went overseas, mostly to the US. A detachable hard-top was made, but it was noisy inside the car and not popular, so a fully enclosed model was built with a high interior standard, the 'Aceca' became one of the most delightful grand touring cars of the period. Demand for the older 2-litre cars fell away to nothing and they were quietly dropped from the catalogue.

The 'Ace' immediately had many racing successes but eventually found itself underpowered when facing cars fitted with Bristol and other more developed engines. Ken Rudd, a Sussex garage owner and part-time racing driver, approached the company suggesting that an 'Ace' fitted with a 2.2 litre Bristol engine, based on a pre-war BMW design, and coupled to the car's outstanding road-holding would be more than a match for the opposition. Thus the highly successful racing 'Ace-Bristol' came to be. The price was a basic £1,340, £240 more than its AC engined predecessor, but unfortunately plus an horrendous 50% tax burden.

The chassis and steering were continuously improved but drum brakes were still fitted in 1956. Rudd raced 'Ace-Bristols' and 'Acecas' with success in Britain and overseas. Unfortunately when doing well in the 1957 Mille Miglia in Italy, which turned out to be the last before being stopped on safety grounds, Tom

1958 Ace-Bristol *Peter Tarplee collection*

Clarke, having overturned his 'Aceca' in practice, punctured the fuel tank in the race and retired. In 1957 Rudd bought a works demonstrator car and modified it for the GP d'Endurance at Le Mans. The Hurlocks declined to do the work saying that they had not made a profit on any of the 'Aces' built to date and could not afford to enter the car themselves. At the end of the race the

1959 Greyhound saloon *Gordon Knowles collection*

AC was tenth overall and second to a Ferrari in its class having averaged 97.98 mph and covered 3,780 km. It was probably the least costly car in the race and the only one which was clearly an un-modified production model. When the Bristol engine went out of production it was Rudd who persuaded AC to fit the Ford straight six 'Zephyr' engine.

The Hurlocks hankered after their traditional markets and in 1955 produced a five-seat saloon, based on an extended 'Aceca' chassis but it did not go into production. Neither did the 'Greyhound' of 1959 have an extended life, although it was a beautiful car offered with AC, Bristol or Ford 'Zephyr Six' engines. Only 82 were made, it really needed a more powerful engine but the car did not get the development it warranted due to being sidelined by the 'Cobra' development programme.

Carroll Shelby was an American racer, who had driven Jaguars and Aston-Martins in Europe and had imported the Ace into the US, and in conjunction with Ford of America produced the prototype 'Cobra Ace' fitted with the new 3.6 litre Ford short-stroke engine and displayed it in New York in 1961. Ford, who needed a sports car to compete with the Chevrolet Corvette saw the possibilities and so Shelby developed the 'Cobra', fitted first with the 4.2 litre Ford engine and then with its 4.7 litre development. Shelby turned up at Thames Ditton with

1963 Cobra *Peter Tarplee collection*

completed drawings and Alan Turner redesigned the 'Ace' chassis to take the new engine, twice as powerful as the AC engine the car had started out with. Disc brakes were standardised. The first Thames Ditton built car fitted with the Ford engine was track-tested at Silverstone on 1 February 1962 by Shelby. The car was shipped to Los Angeles where a development engine and Borg-Warner gearbox was fitted.

Ford and Shelby wanted an out-and-out racer and did not think at all of a road car, whereas the Hurlocks wanted the latter. A compromise was agreed whereby Thames Ditton turned out the chassis and body shells and shipped them to Los Angeles where Shelby married them to the American engine and gearbox and race-tuned the whole machine. Some 100 were built in the first year and in 1963 a number raced successfully in the SCCA 'A' Class . The Chevrolet Corvette was caught flat-footed, it weighed some 1,000 lbs more than the 'Cobra' and did not catch up until it was fitted with a huge 7 litre engine later on.

A 'Cobra' finished 4th at Le Mans in 1964 and in 1966 the ultra-high performance 'Cobra 427' appeared with a Ford 7 litre V-8 engine. A luxury convertible, the 428, was also made at this time with bodywork by Frua of Turin. The prototypes for all these new models were built at Thames Ditton and complete road cars for the markets outside the US were also built there, but the 'hairy' racing models were all built in Los Angeles from chassis and bodyshells supplied from Britain.

In 1973 Derek Hurlock, son of William, who had been instrumental in getting the 428 and 2 litre Cobra into production at Thames Ditton, decided to stop building the 428. There were continual problems in getting the bodies from Italy due to labour disputes there. Then came the oil crisis when a car giving only 16 mpg seemed totally at odds with the world at that time. Production of the invalid carriage stopped in 1976 and it was another difficult time for the company. At the 1973 Motor Show the new mid-engined '3000ME' had been shown as replacement for the 428.

The design of the '3000ME' was influenced by the Lola T-70 CanAm racers designed by Eric Broadley and was a direct competitor to the Ferrari 246GT, at half the price. The new car was a compact rear-engined coupe with a 3 litre Ford engine and the AC designed gearbox in a fabricated sheet-steel chassis clothed by a high-quality glass-fibre body, both built by AC. Derek Hurlock was not impressed with the concept, it was too radical for him, but his designers Alan Turner and Bill Wilson

1973 3000ME *Gordon Knowles collection*

produced a good design that was well received by the technical press. The car was in fact based upon the Maxi-powered 'Diablo' designed by Robin Stables and Peter Bohanna and re-worked for production. The British Leyland transverse 4 cylinder Maxi engine with a 5-speed gear box was a reliable unit but could not, or would not, be produced in the quantities wanted by Thames Ditton. So Alan Turner decided to go for the British Ford ohv 3 litre V6 engine. The gearbox was developed from a Hewland design and used that firm's gear cluster.

The car was provisionally priced at between £3,000 and £4,000 and deliveries were planned to start in June 1974 with production set at 20 per week. 1,200 firm orders were received following the 1974 Motor Show but no firm delivery dates could be set as the company was stopped in its tracks by the need to obtain 'Type Approval' to follow mandatory crash tests. The company finances were low and the delay was fatal, development costs were high as was the implication of the decision to build many components in house, with the outlay on tooling etc. that this called for. By 1976 orders were said to be for 1,400 cars and still no firm delivery dates were forthcoming. 100 sets of components had been bought in from outside suppliers and the new launch date was set for spring 1977 with the price now at £7,000.

After a gestation period of six years and development costs of over £1 million – one estimate was that it was nearer twice that – the 3000ME was at last offered for sale. But what had seemed to be 'state of the art' and very good value in 1973 was another matter in 1979 at a price now of £13,300. Unfortunately the car's road handing was poor, and certainly not up to the usual AC standard. Derek Hurlock personally road-tested the car and, echoing the mind-set of his father and uncle, said in response to an offer of help from the director of a leading sports racing team for a nominal fee of £100; "no thanks, I will decide what steps to take and we will take them ourselves".

In the depths of the recession that had hit British industry at the end of the 1970s it was just not possible to sell enough 3000MEs to break even let alone make any profit. Even moving to smaller premises down the High St. did not help. Derek Hurlock realised that the company and its shareholders did not have the resources to keep going, so he looked for a buyer. A Scottish entrepreneur, David MacDonald, saw an opportunity and bought up the assets including the 3000ME jigs, tools and moulds and set up in a new factory near Glasgow with assistance from the Scottish Development Agency. There were optimistic projections of building 400 cars a year and a development programme was put in hand to use the Alfa Romeo 2.4 litre V6 engine. The money ran out after 30 cars were produced and the Official Receiver arrived in November 1985 after accusations about the company's complex financial affairs.

Next followed a short-lived project by ex BRM Director Aubrey Woods following a move south to Hertfordshire, where the prototype '3000ME Signature' model was built with a Fiat engine. £350,000 was needed to develop the car, but the money was not forthcoming. Once again the AC business was bankrupt.

When AC finished building the 'Cobra' some 1,640 chassis had been completed. In 1974 Brian Angliss, retaining the Surrey connection, formed 'Cobra Parts' to restore cars and to supply spares for the over 1,000 cars still on the road. He set up a small establishment on the Brooklands Estate where he also embarked on building replica 'Cobras' using the original jigs. When he fell foul of the US emission tests he set about building new 'Cobras' to the required specification, retaining the base structure and modifying the superstructure where necessary, particularly by fitting ingenious impact-absorbing front and rear ends on telescopic struts. By 1981 the company had become 'CP Autokraft' and had acquired the AC name. The old business, now 'AC Cars plc.' continued in being, but not in manufacture, still maintaining the Hurlock family interest, its income being solely royalties from 'Autokraft'.

In 1987 the Hurlocks finally relinquished their interest and sold their controlling shares in 'AC Cars plc'. Angliss set up 'AC Cars Ltd.', acquiring 49% of the shares, the remaining 51% were sold to the Ford Motor Co. Subsequently the 49% shareholding of 'AC Cars Ltd.' was bought over by Ford, with Angliss remaining as Managing Director. In 1988 Angliss and Autokraft bought out Ford's holdings and new 90,000 sq. ft premises were taken up at Brooklands and in 1991 the pre-production new 'Ace' was built. In 1993 the 'Ace' went into limited production with a 5 litre Ford V-8 engine. The car was capable of 0–60 mph in 5.7 seconds, and was hand-built on traditional lines with an aluminium-alloy body.

In March 1996 the company once more went into liquidation, and in December yet another new company, 'AC Cars Group Ltd.' was formed, backed by an American, Alan Lubinksy of the Pride Automotive Group Inc. A revised 'Ace' open sports and the new 'Aceca' 4 seat closed coupé together with the 'Super Blower Cobra 212S/C' with a carbon fibre body shell was introduced in 1997. In 2001 the Mamba, a fixed head coupe with a 4 litre straight six engine by Ford of Australia was announced. The firm was then employing about 40 skilled workers and was managed by ex Volvo manager Jan-Erik Jansson. Prices started at £75,000 for the 'Ace' and 'Aceca' and from around £33,000 upwards for the standard 'Cobra'. The 'Super Blower Cobra' started at around £59,000 and was now fitted with the Lotus 350hp twin turbo V-8 engine. The Mamba was due to be available early in 2002, priced from £45,699 to £58,990. All models were built only to firm order.

The company in late 2001, moved again, this time to Frimley, but retained some facilities at Brooklands. In spring of 2002 there was yet another move, to Camberley, following yet more financial difficulties. It was announced in June that year that "the business is in administration and that the Company would enter a company voluntary agreement." It was claimed that more than 80% of AC's £9 million debt was owed to shareholders who remained committed to vehicle production. In late 2002 it was announced by chairman Alan Lubinsky that new funding measures were in hand and that the business was once again being re-structured and that production of the carbon fibre bodied 'Cobra' was being transferred to Malta, but that the aluminium-alloy bodied 'Ace' would continue at Camberley.

(There was no mention of the 'Mamba'). It was stressed that existing retail orders would not be affected by the reorganisation.

It is to be hoped that this famous old name will survive. It is by far the longest-surviving car manufacturer in the county and epitomizes the Surrey motoring style, that of producing small volume, high quality and performance, sports and racing cars. We shall be much the poorer if the name of AC does not continue. The final words in the official company history of 1952 sums it all up, "AC Cars are now one of the very few specialist manufacturers in the United Kingdom, and we shall continue to produce our product as a quality car. Quoting Ruskin, 'There is hardly anything in the world that some man cannot make a little cheaper, and the people who consider price only are this man's lawful prey'".

References

The Dennis archives in the Surrey History Centre, Woking
Dennis, World Trucks No. 6: P Kennet, 1979
75 Years of Dennis Buses & Coaches: Autobus Review (1980)
Fire Engines of Europe: John Creighton, 1980
British Lorries 1900–1992: S W Stevens-Stratten, 1993
The History of AC Cars Ltd.: R G Henderson, 1952
Classic ACs Auto-Carrier to Cobra: John McLellan, 2000
British Car Factories from 1896: Paul Collins & Michael Stratton, 1993
The New Encyclopaedia of Motor Cars: Ed. G N Georgano, 1982
The History of Brooklands Motor Course: William Boddy, 1957

Driving Fast – Post War

Brooklands did not re-open after the Second World War, and there was nowhere to replace it until the wartime airfield at Silverstone in Northamptonshire was rebuilt as a modern Grand Prix circuit and Brands Hatch in Kent was opened. Meantime British car manufacturing got slowly back into production, albeit initially with updated pre-war designs.

A number of Surrey manufacturers of racing and sports cars gradually restarted business, and in some cases started up for the first time. In this chapter, ten of these are reviewed, some were short-lived, others are still with us. They are presented in order of their start-up date.

ALTA, Kingston. 1931 to 1954. Geoffrey Taylor started building cars in his father's stables in Kingston in 1928, fitting his own engine into an ABC chassis. He chose the name Alta, as a contraction of Alberta, simply because he liked the sound of it. In 1931 he formed the Alta Car and Engineering Company and set about designing and building trials, sprints and racing cars. An Alta broke the Brooklands Mountain Circuit class record in 1934. The basic Alta had a 1047cc engine, supplemented in 1935 by 1496 and 1961cc versions. Chassis were now supplied by Rubery Owen to Taylor's design. For 1937 independent coil suspension was introduced and the overall weight reduced. The supercharged 2 litre model produced 180bhp.

In 1945 a revolutionary new engine was announced using a Meehanite block casting, with a light alloy crankcase and head. The chassis had rubber suspension. The car was not an immediate success and its racing debut was delayed until 1948 following development work on it by George Abecassis. The biggest problem was with the two-stage supercharger, but an un-blown engine was successfully fitted in the HWM (qv). In 1952 Alta produced their own Formula 2 car which did not prove competitive. They developed the engine to 2.5 litres for the new Formula 1, but only built one car to this specification. It never raced. The engine was taken up with success by Connaught (q.v).

1938 1961cc Alta, driven by G M Watson at Goodwood in 1952 *National Motor Museum*

The tiny company was always fighting an uphill battle with the racing giants and finally succumbed, concentrating after 1954 on general engineering work.

HRG, Tolworth. 1936 to 1956. The initials came from the names of the founders, E A Halford, G H Robins and H R Godfrey. The cars were intended to carry on the Frazer-Nash tradition of a vintage-style sports car without any frills, though the HRG used bevel drive and not chains, as had the Frazer-Nash. Ron Godfrey, the 'G' in GN Motors, the 'N' was Archie Frazer-Nash, had set up to repair and service GN cars in Richmond after the founders left the business back in 1922. Frazer-Nash went on to build his own rugged sports cars, and HRG continued the tradition in a new factory off the Kingston Bypass. At first the engine was the well-tried 1496cc ohv 4 cylinder Meadows 4ED and the car was fitted with a simple slab-tank, two seat body. It sold for £395 and could reach 90mph. Halford resigned in 1937 to pursue his other interests whilst the marque had considerable success in trials and rallies. In 1938 an HRG was the highest-placed British car at Le Mans. In 1939 Singer engines were introduced and synchromesh gears and coil ignition standardised.

After the war the firm moved up the road to premises that had been occupied by Fox and Nicholls who had been associated with

1.5 litre H R G in the 1937/38 Laurence Cup Trial *National Motor Museum*

Lagonda before the war. There were few changes to the cars though an Aerodynamic 1500 appeared with full-width bodywork, but it was short-lived. Production was set up to build 100 of the streamlined bodies, but although orders came from the USA, Sweden, Africa and Australia, only 31 had been built when the Aerodynamic was withdrawn. A distinguished post-war competition record included the Coupes des Alpes in the 1948 and 1949 Alpine Rallies, class wins in the 1949 and 1950 Production Car Races at Silverstone, and a clean sweep of the 1.5litre class in the 1949 Belgian 24 Hour Race. The success in competition coincided with a drop in sales, only 40 cars were sold in 1948 and a mere 11 in 1950. The traditional HRG survived until 1956, a new prototype with a Vauxhall VX4/90 engine and an aluminium body by Wakefields of East Molesey appeared just before the close, but it was all too late. The last Singer-engined HRG left the factory in July 1956. No more than 240 HRGs of all types were built.

The firm continued as a general engineering business for another ten years but by 1966 the workforce was down to ten and the firm went into liquidation. A supply of spares for the cars was arranged through Trident Garages Ltd. of Ripley. The buildings were sold to the next-door cosmetic manufacturers who promptly demolished them to enable expansion of their own factory.

COOPER, Surbiton and Byfleet. 1948 to 1972. Charles Cooper started up a garage in a builder's yard in Ewell Road, Surbiton in 1920. He had some success with racing and invited Kaye Don to prepare some cars for him. As a result the business moved to a large shed at 243 Ewell Road, Surbiton, which had subsequently to be enlarged at least three times. When his son John returned to the firm after serving during the war as a toolmaker with the Admiralty, the Coopers, father and son, built two 500cc single seat racing cars in 1946 using Fiat Topolino parts and JAP Speedway engines. They proved successful so a company was formed and factory production started in 1948. Among the first drivers was a then young and unknown Stirling Moss who drew attention to himself and the cars by achieving 11 wins in his first season. In 1949 the first two seat sports car was built, the production version having a 1442cc Vauxhall engine. An MG-engined version was successful in rallying and racing, notably driven by Cliff Davis.

The 500cc cars were developed annually throughout the life of Formula 3 and dominated racing until the end of the formula in 1958. The early standard specification included independent suspension by transverse leaf springs and a box-section frame. After 1952 the Mk. VI used a tubular chassis and disc brakes appeared with the Mk. IX. By 1956 360 cars had been built but production of the 500cc models tailed off after then. In 1948 Spike Rhiando put a 1000cc V-twin JAP engine into a Cooper chassis and was remarkably successful in Formula 2. The type dominated hill climbs for many years in the hands of Wharton, Marsh and Boshier-Jones. Between 1951 and 1956 class records were made, mostly at Monza and Montlhéry.

In 1952 the Mk. V chassis was modified and fitted with a front-mounted Bristol 2 litre engine tuned to give 135hp, and later 150hp. Mike Hawthorn's exploits in one of these cars put him in the front rank of Grand Prix drivers leading to his drive with the Ferrari works team. Alternative engines were fitted by several private owners, including Alta, ERA and Maserati. The last front-engined car was a sports model built in 1954 for P N Whitehead with a 'C' type Jaguar engine, and with a 'D' type for 1955.

The real milestone was the sports car change to the rear-fitted 1098cc Coventry Climax engine and a central driving position. A

Mike Hawthorn in a 1953 works Ferrari *Chris Shepheard collection*

space frame was used, retaining the transverse leaf suspension. Transmission was by a reversed Citroën gearbox. The all-enveloping body pioneered the 'shovel-snout' profile that became universal during the 1960s. Cars finished at Le Mans in 1955 and 1956, in which year the 1475 FWB Climax engine was adopted. The next step was the introduction of a Formula 2 version. In 1958, 10 of the 13 races were won by Cooper securing the class Championship for them.

By 1959 the Formula 1 engine had grown to 2462cc, developing 236bhp, and provided Cooper and driver Jack Brabham with their first World Championship. This marked a turning point in Grand Prix car design, all other marques subsequently followed Cooper in adopting the rear-engined approach. In 1960 the GP car was lower, adopted coil suspension and had a 5 speed gearbox. It again won the World Championship. In 1961 Formula 1 was altered to 1.5 litres supercharged, and there was no Climax engine powerful enough to stave off the Ferrari challenge. The success of the Climax engine had been amazing, remembering that it was developed from a wartime design for use in fire pumps.

Meanwhile the sensation of the 1959 Motor Show was the revolutionary front wheel drive Mini introduced by the British

Motor Corporation. The compact small town car concept has since been copied around the world. It was underpriced at below £500 but would have made substantial profits for the company had it been realistically priced. It has been said that not a single Mini ever made a profit for its manufacturer. Cooper had been busy working on the Mini and in 1961 the British Motor Corporation announced the Mini-Cooper series with engines stretched to 997cc, two SU carburetors and front disc brakes. The engine was developed over the years to give eventually 1293cc. There were countless rally and racing successes culminating in Paddy Hopkirk and Henry Lidden winning the Monte Carlo Rally in 1964. The European Rally Championships was also won by the BMC Mini team of Altonen, Mackinon and Hopkirk.

In 1962 the Formula 1 V-8 Climax engine was ready but Cooper and McLaren had only limited success with it. In 1963 it was only in Formula 3, where Stewart's Type 72 won 12 of the 17 races, that success was found. 1965 saw suspension improvements and 1966 a new monocoque was built for the 3 litre Formula 1 using the V-12 Maserati engine.

Charles Cooper had died in 1964 and John had been badly injured in a road accident. In 1965 the racing team moved to the Byfleet Trading Estate. The company merged with the Chipstead Motor Group which had already collected Roy Salvadori's Elmbridge Motors of Tolworth, which itself had absorbed Langley Motors of Thames Ditton and Thomson & Taylor of Cobham. Coopers effectively came to an end in 1969 when the Chipstead Motor Group broke up, racing car production ceasing at this time. John Cooper bought back his name and opened a garage in Sussex. The Byfleet plant continued making Mini-Coopers until 1972 when the works were disposed of to become the Panther car works. Mini-Cooper production was transferred to Longbridge, continuing until October 2000 when the last car was turned out.

When BMW acquired the assets of the Rover business, of which the Longbridge plant had become part, among their plans for new models was a revived Mini, larger and brought up to date, but still recognisably a Mini. When BMW subsequently sold off the Rover business they retained the new Mini design and it is currently in production at the Cowley, Oxford plant. The name is now a recognised brand in its own right, and once again the Mini-Cooper has been resurrected, the handling, road-holding and engine output reminiscent of the earlier models.

The list of racing drivers who drove for Cooper is a roll call of many of the famous names in post war racing. They include: Brabham, Brandon, Bueb, Brown, Collins, Carter, Cooper, Hawthorn, Leston, Lewis-Evans, Macdowell, McLaren, Moss, Rindt, Russell, Salvadori, Surtees and Whitehouse.

CONNAUGHT, Send. 1951 to 1957. Continental Cars Ltd. were established in 1949 by two ex RAF pilots Mike Oliver and Rodney Clarke, and backed by Kenneth McAlpine, to sell imported sports cars, including Bugatti and Alfa Romeo, as well as British makes including Healey and HRG In 1951 the name was changed to Connaught Engineering, derived from 'Continental' and 'Automobile', and production of a sports car was started. It was based on the 14hp Lea Francis with power boosted to 102hp and was fitted with an aerodynamic two-seat body. It was priced at £1,275. A lighter and faster model, the L3, followed but the firm was to make its name with Formula 2 and then Formula 1 racing cars.

The first racer, the Type A for Formula 2, was also based on the 2 litre Lea Francis engine boosted to give 135bhp and had fuel injection, a pre-selector gearbox and independent suspension. In 1954 the Type B Grand Prix car was introduced and was fitted

2 litre Type A Formula 2 Connaught at Goodwood in 1953 *National Motor Museum*

with the Alta 2.5 litre OHC 4 cylinder engine. All-enveloping bodywork was fitted to some cars but it was an unstreamlined version which was responsible for the firm's greatest success. In 1955 Tony Brooks, a young Manchester dental student, who had successfully raced a Formula 2 Connaught for John Riseley-Prichard, became the first British driver in a British car to win a Grand Prix for thirty-one years. How different was the amateur approach in 1955 from the professionalism of today.

Young Brooks had never driven in a Grand Prix and had never driven round the course at Syracuse on the tip of Sicily. Two cars were entered by Connaught, a streamlined one for Les Leston and an unstreamlined one for Brooks. After a brief testing period at Goodwood the cars were loaded into two old converted Green Line AEC buses for the 2,000 miles journey across France and down through Italy, which took longer than anticipated. The buses were impounded at Dunkirk by the French customs as the documentation was incomplete. By the time it was sorted out it was doubtful if they could make it to the circuit for the Friday practice session.

So it proved. Brooks had flown out to Catalonia but had no car to drive round the course and could not afford to hire one. He hired a Vespa scooter and rode it around the course to learn the tricky circuit. The cars finally arrived late Friday night and so the first time that Tony Brooks sat in the car was on the Saturday morning for the qualifying laps. These were restricted by the team in order to ensure that the cars would be alright for the race. There was no spare car and few spare parts, the team could not afford to cater for breakages. In spite of this Brooks qualified third fastest behind the two Maseratis of Musso and Villoresi.

The engines of the two Connaughts were highly stressed and had been tuned to make them competitive so that there were real fears that they would not last the race. After a slow start Brooks caught up with and passed both Maseratis. The crowd thought that the Connaught engine was about to blow up when it emitted a dreadful howl, but it was only the exhaust which had split. Brooks raised the lap record from 99 to 102 mph and won from Musso by almost a minute. It was reported at the time that the organisers had not even considered a win by a car other than an Italian one and had to frantically search for a recording of the British national anthem to play at the prize-giving ceremony.

Unfortunately this wonderful win was not to be repeated. A 1.5 litre sports car ran unsuccessfully at Le Mans in 1955 but the cost of running a Grand Prix racing team before the days of corporate sponsorship proved too much for the little company and in 1957 it closed down and the cars were sold. Only 46 cars were built at Send, 30 sports cars, 9 Formula 2 racers and 7 Grand Prix cars.

The site became an ordinary garage with a Shell forecourt for some years until a new filling station was built at the nearby roundabout. It was not completely the end of building racing cars on the site for in 1960–61 the Emeryson Company, formerly of Twickenham, built a few Formula Junior cars there in conjunction with Connaught. In later years the site became a used car lot, then a builder's yard, and gradually became run down. Mike Oliver returned to flying, becoming Chief Test Pilot for Folland and helped to develop the little Gnat fighter/trainer whilst Tony Brooks went on to drive for BRM, Vanwall and Ferrari, competing in a further 38 Grand Prix, of which he won six. He shared another historic all-British first, the first Formula One World Championship win, with Stirling Moss in a Vanwall at Aintree in 1957, and went on to win the Belgian, French, German (twice) and Italian Grand Prix. He was third in the driver's championship in 1958 and second in 1959. He retired in 1961.

What of the famous Syracuse car? It returned there in 1957 with Les Leston as driver, but broke a driveshaft during practice, the flailing shaft split open the fuel tank whose nitro-methane contents spilled out onto the hot exhaust. The car was burned out but the chassis was salvaged and was sold off when the firm closed the same year. It was sold with sufficient 'bits' to rebuild the car, passing eventually to one H Jones, an army officer who never found the time to work on the car. He later became famous as Col. H Jones VC during the Falklands war. Subsequently the car passed into the hands of Bernie Ecclestone, the Formula 1 impresario, who has had the car completely rebuilt and it is now in his collection of racing cars in his private museum. Ecclestone had owned and raced Connaughts in his earlier days.

The old workshops at Send were demolished in late 1999 after a farewell party had been held in the forecourt by the developers for members of the Connaught Club and other devotees. A new office building, Connaught House, now stands on the site. A plaque by the front door briefly describes how the building got its name.

HWM, Walton-on-Thames. 1950 to 1956. George Abecassis had made a name for himself driving pre-war Alta racing cars. After the war he teamed up with John Heath to form Hersham and

Walton Motors. Both Abecassis and Heath raced Altas in the late 1940s as well as running the garage business and over the winter of 1948–49 they had started building their own version of the Alta using the 2 litre Alta engine in a new chassis of their own design with independent rear suspension. The car was designed to compete in sports car events and could be stripped down for Formula 2 races, and would at the same time be perfectly usable on the public road. The front suspension and stub axles were Standard 14, Citroën provided the rack and pinion steering and the first car's rear axle was from a spare pre-war Lagonda Rapier unit. The engine was not new but transferred from the Alta that Abbecassis had raced, it was now coupled to an ENV pre-selector gearbox. The team raced this car alongside a new GP Alta driven by John Heath. By 1950 a team of four Formula 2 racing cars had been built led by a young Stirling Moss. There was now no pretence that the cars would be driven on the road or in sports car events, although they had been designed with that concept still in mind. They now had front coil spring suspension, based on the MG TD, Morris Minor steering replacing the Citroën, and a de Dion rear end suspension. 1951 was a successful year and in 1952 the team achieved a 1–2–3 victory in the International Trophy at Silverstone. These cars had twin ohc 2.5 litre 4 cylinder engines and now all-round independent suspension and pre-selector gearboxes.

Other successes followed including that of Paul Frere winning the Grand Prix des Frontieres at Chimay. Although money was always a problem, in 1953 a 3.4 litre Jaguar Mk. 7 engine and synchromesh gearbox was married to the HWM chassis in a sports car which was built in small numbers. John Heath was tragically killed driving an HWM Jaguar in the 1956 Mille Miglia. With the loss of one of the founders and the continuing financial problems the racing business folded. The firm continued in business selling and servicing sports cars, including the exotic Facel Vega and Iso Rivolta models.

TYRRELL, Ockham. 1959 to 1998. Ken Tyrrell, known to all as 'Chopper' from his connections with the family timber-hauling and tree surgeons business, bought himself a racing car in 1951. He raced throughout the fifties becoming a leader of the Formula 2 league. He became manager briefly of the Cooper-BMC Formula Junior Team but soon afterwards, in 1959, he set up his own racing business, the Ken Tyrrell Racing Team, in the family timberyard.

Ken discovered the young Jackie Stewart who started racing Formula 3 Coopers for Ken in 1964. In 1968 he entered Formula 1 with Matra-Fords to his own modifications. He used Ford Cosworth engines exclusively in these cars and in those designed by Derek Gardner and built himself after 1960. Stewart had instant success for Tyrrell winning the World Championship with the Matra-Ford in 1969. For the 1971 season Gardner designed a pioneering car with a wide, flat nose which hid the air intakes. It was potentially a success and gained Ken all important sponsorship. The car won seven races that year, six of them driven by Stewart, winning the driver's championship for him. He repeated the success in 1973 again driving Tyrrell. In 1971 Tyrrell had also won the Constructors' Championship and was

Ken Tyrrell with his new Tyrrell Ford 007 in 1974 *National Motor Museum*

second in 1973. Stewart then retired from active racing but has remained very involved with the sport ever since, first with his own racing car, which he sold on to Ford and is now raced under the Jaguar name. He then became Chairman of the British Racing Drivers' Club, the owners of Silverstone, and was active in 2003 in attempts to ensure the continuation of the circuit as a Grand Prix venue. Along the way he received a knighthood for his contributions to British motor sport.

After Stewart's departure Tyrrell had fewer successes. The Swedish driver Ronnie Petersen had been successful alongside Stewart and in 1974 the South African Jody Scheckter won the British Grand Prix for Tyrrell. For the 1976 season Gardner brought out a most remarkable design, a six-wheeled car, which combined low drag and high cornering potential. An added bonus was excellent braking through larger disc brake surface areas. Many were sceptical about the car's chances, but Jody Scheckter and Patrick Depailler brought the six-wheelers home in first and second places in the Swedish Grand Prix. The FIA rules were changed for the 1978 season and the Tyrrell, now designed by Maurice Phillipe, had the regulation fuel bags meaning the chassis design was radically different. Also engines with more than 12 cylinders were banned, and the fuel bags were not allowed to carry more than 250 litres. High aerofoil wings and high air boxes were also banned. By this time all F1 cars were adopting front and rear wings which helped improve stability and cornering. However good the new Tyrrell was, and it was acknowledged to be an excellent design, the 'ground effect' cars, as demonstrated by the Chapparal and Lotus, ultimately destroyed its superiority.

In the 1980's carbon fibre bodies were fashionable and the 'ground effect' along with sliding skirts was effectively outlawed by the need for a flat-bottomed car with only four wheels. This ended the Tyrrell hopes of further developing the six-wheeled car programme. By 1986 the regulations had been changed again so that only turbo-charged engines were allowed. In 1987 cars with an engine below 3.5 litres capacity had to have it turbo-charged, but above that figure engines could be normally aspirated. The 1990 Tyrrell car, designed now by Harvey Postlewaite, introduced the high nose and the anhedral front wing, that is one with a curved top but flat underneath. The regulations now called for engines limited to 3 litres capacity, normally aspirated, whilst wing sizes were reduced to slow the cars down.

Tyrrell was in the forefront of the new technology introduced in the 1990's, finger tip controls for changing the gears, and the use of carbon fibre and kevlar components. Engine management systems which send a constant stream of data from the car to the pits on the health of the engine, gearbox and chassis and communication systems that allow the driver and his pit crew to speak to each other during a race became universally adopted during the decade.

Ken Tyrrell, now well into his seventies and with failing health, finally decided to call it a day and in 1998 sold the business to BAR (British American Racing) and so finally broke the tradition of the 'Racing Cars from the Woodyard'. Many of the engineering staff joined the new Honda Racing Developments team, a small number moving to the new BAR headquarters in Brackley. Ken was subsequently diagnosed as having cancer and died in 2000, marking the end of a remarkable era. Apart from Stewart, Scheckter, Peterson and Depailler, other Tyrrell drivers included Jean Alesi, Mika Salo and Jos Verstappen.

CATERHAM, Caterham and Crayford, Kent. 1973 to date. As well as producing racing cars Surrey has always been in the forefront of building fast sports cars. Not many are faster than the remarkable Caterham Seven. Colin Chapman introduced the Lotus 'Super Seven' sports car in 1957 with a spaceframe chassis and a simple, some would say minimal, aluminium panelled body and cycle style wings. The car was designed primarily as a road-going sports car rather than a racing car. The buyer Colin Chapman had in mind would drive the car to work in the week and then at the weekend use it in the less serious forms of motor sport – hillclimbs, sprints and club racing. But first and foremost it was designed for the road. Edward Lewis took delivery of the first pre-production Seven in time for the September 1957 Brighton Speed Trials. He had a few problems on his first run and nearly ended up in the sea. His second attempt was much better and he recorded 29.72 seconds to win his class. Lewis then took the car to Prescott where he won the 1,100cc sports car class. Lewis competed for two seasons in the Seven fitting it with a 1,500cc Coventry Climax engine for 1958. He then sold the car for £900, less the engine.

The first production car was delayed whilst development work on the new Elite was completed in readiness for the Earls Court Motor Show. For the Seven, less costly components, including the engine, were designed and fitted. The Climax engine was out as were disc brakes. Chapman went back to his drawing board and produced a live-axled Seven with drum brakes and a Ford 1172cc side-valve engine. The car went into production late 1957 and in kit form was offered at £536. Chapman set up a number of 'Lotus Centres' to sell the Elite and the Seven. Anthony Crook ran a garage and filling station in Station Road Caterham during the 1950s. Crook left in 1959 to head up Bristol Cars and the Caterham business was taken over by a group headed by Graham Nearn who approached Chapman to become a Lotus Centre. Soon the deal was done, in a completely non-businesslike manner, the only commitment was for Caterham to buy an Elite kit and a Seven kit. "No sales targets or anything like that", Nearn subsequently said. "It was simply a question of here's a couple of cars, get on with it." Caterham was set up as a selling agent for just this one brand and were one of the first authorised dealers for this remarkable sports car which could be bought complete or as a kit of parts for home assembly. In 1961 the market contracted and Lotus imposed an arbitrary price – and profit – cut on the Seven. Caterham still sold the occasional new Seven but concentrated on the second-hand and spares market, setting up deals with an insurance company and a finance house, thus being able to offer suitable facilities to prospective buyers. In 1962 Caterham sold off the forecourt business to Esso when the partners split up, Graham Nearn becoming sole owner of the premises behind the petrol forecourt. Nearn set up a car body repair business, Caterham Coachworks, which was the true forerunner of the Caterham Seven.

By 1966 it was clear that Lotus were concentrating on other more advanced sports car designs, as well as Formula 1 racing cars, parts became difficult to obtain and whilst Lotus had not officially dropped the Seven, since they had moved into a new factory at Hethel in Norfolk they had simply not restarted building it after the move. Nearn approached Chapman at the Racing Car Show in January 1967, who seemed surprised that there was still a demand for the car. Nearn had protracted negotiations with David Lazenby, who was running the components side of Lotus, and arranged to buy the parts available to build 20 S2-1500 Sevens. Caterham then negotiated the sole selling rights for the Super Seven in Britain from 1967. In 1971 the end of the Lotus Seven appeared more and more imminent in spite of the introduction of the S4 which was only being produced half-heartedly by Lotus. Nearn obtained a commitment from Chapman that year to buy out all the rights,

143

jigs and tools as and when Lotus finally decided to pull out of Seven production. In 1973 Caterham Cars paid an undisclosed sum to Lotus to take over the sole manufacturing rights for the Seven and also the Formula Ford racing cars and more than 50 Lotus Twin-Cam engines. There had been a competitive bid from the New Zealand firm of Steele Brothers who obtained two sets of moulds and jigs and a three year licence. They only built a few cars before the project faltered.

Production was started in the garage in Caterham in 1974 and the car continues to have a successful and enduring life till today. The early Caterhams were the S3 model fitted with the Twin-Cam Lotus engines that had been obtained as part of the deal. The car had a blistering performance with a top speed of 114mph and reached 60mph in 6.2 seconds, whilst retaining the lightning handling response associated with the Lotus produced cars. Before the Lotus Twin-Cam engine supply finally ran out a Ford 1600GT Kent engine was fitted and subsequently became a significant component for many years. Commercial components were used wherever practical, Triumph Spitfire front hubs, Morris Ital rear axles and differentials for example at the beginning. In 1984 Caterham built the Jubilee Seven with a high standard of equipment to commemorate the 25 year association with the model.

The Seven, in spite of Chapman's original target market being the driver who used the car for work and 'less serious racing at the weekend', became highly successful in serious motor sporting events. The obvious class for the cars to race in was the 1172cc formula sponsored by the 750 Motor Club. Soon objections were raised by competitors in other makes and as early as 1959 the 750 Club revised the rules so as exclude all but the basic Seven. In 1961 Sevens ran in 'the waifs and strays' class F, but the next year the Seven America was placed in Production Class G and the Super Seven in Class D. In both classes the Sevens dominated and paid the penalty by the next year being reclassified against much stronger opposition. The SCCA then decided that it did not want the Seven at all after the special SCCA 1340cc engine was developed.

By 1973, when Caterham took over production, the Seven had competed successfully in many events and classes over the years, in basic and developed forms. By then sports-car racing had become more specialised: the Seven was no longer the all-round racer it had been a decade before. Production Sports Car racing was instigated that year to cater for true road-going sports cars as

144

distinct from highly developed Modified Sports Cars who now had their own category. After the changeover of Seven production to Caterham the RAC was reluctant to admit it to either category. Nearn was insistent and for the 1975 season the Seven appeared in the list of Modsports in spite of objections. Nearn said at the time, "I argued that the Seven was a production car, a sports car and therefore it was entitled to race; the fact that it was quick and competitive was too bad, certainly no reason it shouldn't race."

Nearn and fellow director David Wakefield were often to be seen on the track at this time, Brands Hatch being a favourite venue. It was said that Nearn would 'borrow' a car from the Caterham showroom for the weekend taking it back on Monday morning hopefully none the worse for its high-speed adventure. By 1980 the Seven was at last pronounced eligible for British Production Sports Car racing, following this many Sevens again took to the track. In 1983 a Seven won the 750 Club's Silverstone Six Hours, Tony Dron and Gary White winning on handicap. In 1984 Maynard Soares won the Production Sports Car Championship and the same year a Seven, driven by Clive Roberts, Richard Cleare and Jeremy Coulter ran strongly in Britain's only 24 hour race until pushed off the track by another competitor. In 1985 sports car racing regulations were relaxed to cover 'road-going cars' and Robin Gray in his Lotus Twin-Cam powered Seven won virtually every event he entered.

The firm won a court case against Westfield Cars who were producing a similar car, also based on the Lotus Super Seven, and which was largely sold as a kit car. Caterham claimed successfully that it had the sole rights to manufacture and market the original Lotus design. Westfield climbed down and modified their design with enough differences to avoid charges of plagiarism and infringement of copyright. The Westfield SEi started production in 1987, the same year that Caterham, in need of larger premises, moved production of the Seven to a new factory at Crayford in Kent, retaining the marketing operations in Caterham.

The car has been in production now for almost fifty years, thirty as the Caterham, and although it has gone through many improvements in that time, is still fundamentally the same spartan and relatively simple car that Colin Chapman designed all those years ago. Apart from engine upratings and road-holding improvements to match, the biggest visual difference came in 2000 when the Roadsport V model was introduced. It is

HRH Prince Edward and Lord Montagu in the Caterham Super 7 at Beaulieu which was first prize in the 1992 raffle *National Motor Museum*

slightly wider and longer than the original design, though still without doors and with only minimal bad weather equipment. The basic engine was a 1600cc twin-carburettor Ford engine, although the Roadsport V is fitted with a 120bhp, 1.6 litre MG X-Power engine and a five speed gearbox. The basic model can still be bought in kit form as well as a complete car, in the former guise for a sum of around £10,000. The days of the £500 Lotus Seven kit has long gone. The Roadsport has a 0 to 60 time of only 6 seconds, less than many super sports cars costing twice or three times the money, although undoubtedly these will give the driver greater comfort. From time to time Caterham produce limited-edition cars and in 2003, to celebrate the car's 30th anniversary, just 15 each of two variants were built. The Tracksport is an out and out track-day car with a race-tuned MG X-Power 1.8 litre engine developing 140 bhp, it will reach 60 mph in 5.3 seconds and has a maximum speed of 122mph. The car is fitted with a race seat and five-point racing harness and a wide track front suspension. It was available in one colour only – a vivid green – and cost £17,950. The SV30 is based on the longer wheelbase Seven and has the 1.6 litre MG engine. It has, by Caterham standards, such luxury fittings as leather seats, alloy wheels and full weather equipment. A luxury model indeed, costing £19,950.

Around 5,000 Lotus and Caterham Sevens have been built, a surprising large number are still on the road. There is a keen second-hand market and any particular model is likely to be available somewhere but perhaps difficult to find. The Caterham is a remarkable performer by any standards, but the driver needs to be young and agile in mind and body to even contemplate getting in and out. The passenger needs to be equally so and aware in advance of what he or she is letting themselves in for when climbing aboard.

BRABHAM (Motor Racing Developments Ltd.), Chessington. 1962 to 1989

Milton Keynes. 1990 to 1992. The rapid rise of the Brabham Formula 1 racing car was one of the features of the sixties racing scene. Jack Brabham was an Australian who became world champion in both 1959 and 1960 driving Coopers on both occasions. He followed this by becoming world champion once more in 1966, this time in a car of his own design. He was the first, and so far only driver, to win the world title driving a car of his own design. He was followed as champion in 1967 by Denny Hulme and by Nelson Piquet in 1981 and 1983 driving Brabhams.

Brabham went back to Australia after winning for Cooper in 1960 and met Ron Tauranac, an aircraft engineer. They struck up a friendship and moved to England where they set up Motor Racing Developments, the first cars being badged MRD. Brabham was persuaded to put his own name on the car as MRD did not translate very well into French and the first success came in 1964. For the 1.5 litre formula that year Coventry Climax engines were used, wins being scored by the American driver Dan Gurney in France and Mexico. Earlier Brabham had had equal success in Formula Junior racing in 1963, and had the same year built a successful sports model, the BT5. By 1964 Brabhams were running in Formula 1, Formula 2, Formula 3 and at Indianapolis. Brabham, driving a BT 8 sports car fitted with a 2 litre Coventry Climax engine won the 1965 Tourist Trophy race.

It was also in 1965 that Brabham started selling F1 chassis to other drivers, including Rob Walker and Bob Anderson. For the 1966 new 3-litre Formula 1 a V-8 engine was developed by

Tauranac in conjunction with the Australian REPCO company. Brabham won his first race in his own car, the French Grand Prix, and went on to win his third World Title and the Constructors' Championship. Jack Brabham then partially withdrew from racing but in 1967 Denny Hulme repeated the former's success of the previous year, winning both the Drivers' Championship and that of the Constructors' for Brabham. For 1967 Hulme moved to McLaren and Brabham signed up the Austrian driver Jochen Rindt, but the REPCO engine was not up to the task, Rindt leaving at the end of the season to join Lotus.

The 1970 season was to be Jack's last. Money was short and results poor, although he won the South African Grand Prix at the start of the season and almost won at Monaco, going off during the last lap. At the end of the year Jack Brabham retired and returned to Australia. He sold the company to Tauranac, but the team did not do well, drivers Graham Hill and Tim Schenken scoring only five points between them. The cars did better in Formula 2, Carlos Reutemann finishing second in the European Championship. At the start of the 1972 season Tauranac sold out to Bernie Ecclestone who did not have a good first season with Hill and Reutemann as drivers. For 1973 the South African Gordon Murray was promoted to be chief designer and produced the BT42, driven by Reutemann and Wilson Fittipaldi. No wins were recorded but Brabham finished fourth in the World Championship.

The BT44 was raced in 1974 by Reutemann and among others, Carlos Pace. Although Reutemann won three races the team slipped to fifth in the Constructors' Title race. For 1975 sponsorship was obtained from Martini and Reutemann and Pace each won a race and enough other placings to give the team second place in the Championship, with Reutemann third and Pace sixth in the Drivers' Championship. The team then linked up with Alfa Romeo for 1976 who produced a flat-12 engine to power the new BT45 car. The new car was not a success and Reutemann left at the end of the season to join Ferrari. He was replaced for 1977 by John Watson. The season got off to a good start when Pace was second in Argentina, but unfortunately soon after the South African race he was killed in a flying accident. Hans Stuck was hired as his replacement, but he and Watson scored only three podium finishes.

For 1977 Parmalat replaced Martini as sponsors and Murray designed the remarkable BT45, an angular design with surface cooling. This did not work and the car was substantially revised,

Watson finished third on the car's debut in South Africa. The ground-effect Lotus was the dominant car that year and Murray came up with his own version, producing the BT46B, known as the Fan Car, which as well as cooling the engine created a partial vacuum under the car. Lauda won the Swedish GP but soon after the car was banned by the sport's governing body, the FIA. The car was revised once more and as the BT46C was driven to victory by Lauda in Italy. The team finished third in the Constructors' Championship.

Watson moved to McLaren and Nelson Piquet was signed to replace him for 1978. There was a new V-12 engine from Alfa Romeo but the BT49 cars were unreliable. The Italians were planning their own car so Brabham switched engines to Cosworth in a revised BT49, Piquet winning three races during 1980. The following year he also had three wins and a string of good finishes gave him the World Championship. For 1981 BMW engines were used but it was not a good season. In 1983 pitstop re-fuelling was reintroduced and Piquet and Riccardo Patrese drove the new BT53, Piquet had three victories again taking the World Championship. Patrese won one race and the team took the Constructor's Championship. 1984 was not a good season, Piquet won twice but the cars were unreliable. For 1985 new sponsors in Olivetti and Pirelli appeared, Piquet scoring an unexpected win in France.

There were big changes for 1986, Piquet left to join Williams and Patrese was joined by Elio de Angelis. Murray designed the BT55, the 'Skateboard', so called because the BMW engine was tilted at an angle. The engine and its Weismann gearbox were unreliable and mid-season de Angelis was killed testing at the Paul Ricard circuit in France. Derek Warwick replaced him but the cars did not do well. Ecclestone seemed to be losing interest, concentrating more on the sale of F1's TV rights. Murray moved to McLaren and for 1987 the BT56 was designed by David North, John Baldwin and Sergio Rinland. The BMW laydown engines had to be used as all the old upright units had been sold off. Money was again short and Patrese moved to Williams at the end of the year. BMW also withdrew and Ecclestone announced that Brabham would be taking a sabbatical year.

The team built a Procar for Alfa Romeo but then Ecclestone sold out to Swiss businessman Joachim Luhti. The BT58 was designed in a hurry by Rinland with a Judd V-8 engine and Pirelli tyres for 1989. Martin Brundle and Stefano Modena scored eight points between them but then Luhti was arrested on fraud charges mid-season and the team foundered. Luhti agreed that Mike Earle and Joe Chamberlain could run the operation but the sale was blocked by Peter Windsor who had injunctions to stop the team being sold as he had been involved with Luhti's original purchase but had been excluded from the deal with Earle and Chamberlain.

Martin Brundle walked out and a new buyer appeared. Windsor agreed to the sale to the Middlebridge Group who moved the operation to Milton Keynes. David Brabham, son of the founder, joined as driver with Modena, but the team struggled during 1990. For 1991 a deal was struck with Yamaha to supply engines and Brundle was re-engaged to drive alongside Mark Blundell. The pair collected three points between them, but money was once again short. At the end of the season Yamaha switched to Jordan and Brabham were left with Judd engines, old cars and no money.

The team borrowed heavily from Landhurst Leasing and started 1992 with Eric van de Poele and the female driver Giovanna Amati, who was later replaced by Damon Hill. They managed to qualify in only three races and in midseason the team finally quit for good. The end of thirty interesting and not unprofitable years.

McLAREN, 1964–1980 Croydon.
McLAREN INTERNATIONAL, 1980–1984 Woking.
TAG McLAREN Group, 1984 to date Woking. Bruce McLaren was born in New Zealand, he came to Britain in 1958 and was paid £60 to race a Cooper at Aintree. In December 1959 at Sebring, USA, he became the youngest driver to win a World Championship Grand Prix, again in a Cooper, retaining that distinction until 2003. In 1960, still in a Cooper, he came second to Jack Brabham in the World Championship and was third in 1962. In 1963 he founded his own team, and in 1964 linked up with Peter Agg of Trojan to build a sports racer and then a F1 car which appeared on the grid in 1966.

In the early 1960s Trojan of Croydon had bought the Elva Sports Car Company and built the Elva Courier sports car and Elva racing cars. The first McLaren/Agg car was the M1, a sports racer with a 355bhp 4.5 litre V-8 Oldsmobile engine. Graham Hill, Chris Amon and Dan Gurney were drivers of the car in the Can-Am (Canada & American) 1964 series. In 1965 Robin Herd was hired to design the F1 car, the body shell was built of Mallite, an aerospace material formed from plywood and aluminium sheeting. The first car had an Oldsmobile V-8 engine and subsequently was run in 1966 fitted with Ford or Serenissima engines. It was not a success. The M3 was a single seater sportscar which raced in hill-climbs and Formula Libre.

McLaren's success in Can-Am began in 1966 with the M6A, powered by a 4-litre Chevrolet engine. McLaren and Denny Hulme won five of the first six races in the series and finished first and second in the Championship. The M4B with a BRM engine was raced in F1 by Piers Courage. In 1968 the M8 with a 7-litre Chevrolet engine came first and second in the Can-Am series. With the arrival of the Cosworth DFV engines, Herd designed a new F1 car, the M7, for 1968. It was raced by McLaren, winning the Race of Champions and the Belgian Grand Prix, whilst Hulme won the Italian and Canadian events. To cope with the increased demand for cars a new factory was opened in Beddington Lane, Croydon.

In 1969 a new car with aerofoils again came first and second in the Can-Am series, while various versions of the M7 ran in F1 races. The M9A was a four-wheel-drive car which was raced by Derek Bell at the British Grand Prix. For 1970 the team planned to race the M14A in F1, a revised M8 for Can-Am and also to enter Indycar racing. Unfortunately McLaren was killed whilst testing the M8 at Goodwood, but despite this sad loss Hulme went on to win the series once more. Teddy Mayer took over control of the team and kept up the momentum. Gordon Coppuck designed the M16 Indycar, Ralph Bellamy the M19 F1 car and revised versions of the Can-Am and F5000 cars. Apart from Hulme's success John Cannon won the F5000 title but there were no wins in F1 or Indycars.

For 1972 Hulme and Peter Revson drove Yardley sponsored M19s, Hulme winning in South Africa. The pair also raced in Can-Am and dominated it, with Revson winning the title. The revised M16 began to win Indy races in the Penske run team and there was a F2 car for rising star Jody Scheckter. For one year, in 1973, Trojan ran their own racing team, then in 1974 the team was split, with Teddy Mayer running the F1 Marlboro Texaco team with drivers Emmerson Fittipaldi and Hulme, whilst Phil Kerr ran Mike Hailwood in a Yardley McLaren. Jochen Mass took over when Hailwood broke a leg, Fittipaldi gave the team its first world title.

Hulme retired at the end of the season, his place being taken by Mass. At the end of 1975 Fittipaldi moved to the Copersucar funded team and he was replaced by James Hunt, who won the

1976 world title driving a revised M23 car. For 1978 Mass was replaced by Patrick Tambay, but the M26 was not a competitive car. By 1980 the team had withdrawn from Indy racing to concentrate on F1 with drivers John Watson and Alain Prost. In mid-season sponsors Marlboro engineered a merger with Ron Dennis's Project Four Racing which had also run in F2 under Marlboro colours. Dennis and Mayer became joint managing directors of McLaren International whilst Coppuck joined March. The team moved into a new, larger, factory in Woking. They have subsequently moved once more into new palatial premises, still in Woking. Ron Dennis had served his apprenticeship with Thomson and Taylor of Cobham and had spent all his working life with racing and sports cars, first with Cooper and then with Brabham before setting up his own F2 team. John Barnard was appointed technical director and designed the MP4/1, the first carbon fibre composite car in F1. Prost left to join Renault and was replaced by Andre de Cesaris for 1981, he had a string of accidents but Watson won the British Grand Prix in an MP4/1.

Dennis persuaded retired world champion Niki Lauda to make a comeback and he joined Watson for 1982, Lauda winning at Long Beach and at Brands Hatch and Watson in Belgium and Detroit. Mayer left the team at the end of the year, Dennis becoming sole Managing Director. For 1983 Ford engines, which did not prove to be a success due to unreliability, were used until the TAG-funded Porsche turbo-engines were ready. 1984 proved to be a highly successful season, Prost returning in place of Watson, and the team had great success winning 12 races with Lauda winning the Drivers' Championship by half a point from Prost. Barnard's MP4/2 design had given the team the most resounding success yet seen in F1. At the end of the year Mansour Ojjeh of TAG took a 60% shareholding in the team with Dennis taking up the remaining 40%.

The 1985 title went to Prost with the team winning a second Constructors' title but Lauda finally retired at the end of the season. For 1986 Keke Rosberg joined the team, but had a poor season, meanwhile Prost won a second title. In 1987 Stefan Johannson joined Prost who again won the World Title, but by now the car was proving less competitive, made worse by Barnard moving to Ferrari at the end of the season. For 1988 McLaren joined up with Honda as engine suppliers with Prost and Ayrton Senna as drivers. Senna won the title with eight wins, Prost coming second with seven. 1989 saw the rules changed to

Alain Prost in a Mclaren-Honda at Silverstone 1988 *National Motor Museum*

allow only normally-aspirated engines, but Senna won six Grand Prix with the new Honda V-10 engined car, Prost won only four but took the World Title after a controversial collision with Senna at Suzuka.

Meanwhile, also in 1989, the F1 high performance road car was designed by Gordon Murray and built to be the fastest and best sports car in the world. His target was to make the car as compact and as light as possible, he achieved a weight of 2205 lbs. He wanted an atmospheric engine that would give immediate response and develop at least 550hp. Honda were supplying engines for the race cars so it seemed obvious to turn to them for the F1 engine, but they declined. So Murray turned to his old friend Paul Rosch at BMW who produced the all-aluminium 6.1 litre V-12 engine developing 627hp. The F1 body was made of carbon-fibre composites mainly in an aluminium honey-comb sandwich. The front end of the car was designed as an energy-absorbing structure, the F1 is the only road-going car that has survived a 30mph barrier crash test without incurring any structural damage.

It was initially planned to produce 500 cars at a rate of 50 per year, all to individual order, but after 150 were made production was halted. At around £530,000 the car was one of the most expensive

The McLaren F1 on display at the National Motor Museum, Beaulieu 1990 *National Motor Museum*

production cars ever built. The three-seat car, has the driver in the middle to provide a Formula 1 feel, and the passengers to each side and slightly behind the driver to evenly distribute the weight. The car was claimed to be the fastest road car ever built and it took some 2250 man hours to hand-build each one.

Prost left the team to join Ferrari and was replaced by Gerhard Berger for 1990, when Senna won six races and the team's third consecutive World title. For 1991 Honda built a new V-12 engine and Senna won another Drivers' title with the team beating Williams for the Constructors' Championship. 1992 was less successful with Senna finishing fourth in the Drivers' Championship with McLaren second in the Constructors'. Honda announced at the end of the year that they were withdrawing from F1. Dennis signed Michael Andretti to replace Berger who had moved to Ferrari to work with John Barnard. Ford HB engines fitted with TAG management systems were used after attempts to buy Ligier's Renault V-10 supply failed. In 1993 a three-man team was announced; Senna, Andretti and Mikka Hakkinen. The latter did most of the testing and only drove in three races at the end of the season, replacing Andretti. The car was more successful than anticipated due to a combination of Senna's driving and an effective active suspension system. Senna won five races but moved to Williams at the end of the season.

McLaren dallied with running a car with a V-12 Lamborghini engine but instead signed a four-year deal with Peugeot. Hakkinen and Martin Brundle drove but positive results were few. At the end of the year Dennis negotiated his way out of the Peugeot deal and linked up with Mercedes-Benz to supply engines, from whom McLaren still obtain their engines today. In 1995 the team re-entered sports car racing with a version of the F1 road car. It was highly successful, being the dominant team in GT racing and winning the Le Mans 24 hours at the first attempt in 1995 with Dalmas, Lehto and Sekiya as drivers. The Formula 1 programme was not so successful, former World Champion Nigel Mansell had to postpone his debut in the MP4/10B as he could not fit into the cockpit. He was disappointing when he did eventually race and was replaced by Mark Blundell. Hakkinen had a big accident in Adelaide, suffering a fractured skull.

1996 saw Hakkinen partnered by David Coulthard but results were disappointing, at the end of the year Marlboro left after 23 years of sponsoring the team. Dennis signed a deal with the German tobacco company, West, and for 1997 the cars appeared in Mercedes silver. The team struggled but at Jerez Hakkinen was controversially handed victory by Coulthard following an accident involving Villeneuve and Michael Schumacher. For 1998 and 1999 Hakkinen proved the more competitive of the two drivers securing the World Championship in both years. McLaren also won the Constructors' Championship in 1998 but came second to Ferrari the next year.

In April 1998 McLaren had taken their 5-year old F1 road car to the Ehra-Leissen test track in Germany where the virtually standard V-12 car reached 240.1mph setting a new record. In 1993 the car had taken the record at 231mph from a modified Jaguar XJ220 in Italy, where it had reached 213mph. In mid 1999 it was announced that Daimler Chrysler AG was to take up a 40% shareholding in the team, 30% from Ojjeh and 10% from Dennis. The deal included plans for a new road car to be designed by Gordon Murray and to be called the Mercedes-Benz SLR McLaren and was due to go into production in 2003. (SLR equals sport-light-racing).

It duly appeared in public for the first time at the Goodwood Festival in July 2003 and subsequently at the Frankfurt Motor Show. McLaren are responsible for the suspension design, aerodynamics and handling; AMG provide the 5,439cc, 617bhp supercharged V-8 engine with dashboard-selectable transmission, and the five-speed automatic gearbox with manual-shift options, whilst Mercedes are responsible for styling and packaging. The SLR is the first series production car to have a carbon-fibre unitary chassis/bodyshell. It takes just 3.8 seconds to reach 62mph and a total of 28.8 to top 186mph before running out of further power at 208mph. The car handles as a McLaren should, but has the ambience and comfort one would expect from a Mercedes costing £313,465. It is planned to build 500 cars a year for the next seven years. Delivery of the first of the new cars was scheduled for spring 2004 but quoted delivery at the end of 2003 was three years, such already is the demand!

The Formula 1 team failed to compete with Ferrari in 2000 and 2001 and Mikka Hakkinen retired at the end of the year. For 2002 another Finn, Kimi Raikkonen joined Coulthard and came the closest to beating Ferrari and Schumacher who dominated again. In 2003 Raikkonen again was the more successful of the McLaren drivers but the team trailed behind Ferrari and Williams in both the Drivers' and Constructors' championships. The company provides skilled employment in Woking and continues the Surrey tradition of building high-quality, high-performance, racing and sports cars.

LISTER, 1983 to date. Leatherhead. The Lister company was an old established general engineering business based in Cambridge. In 1954 Brian Lister built a sports-racing car powered by a Bristol engine. Archie Scott-Brown drove the car to success in a number of events including the supporting race to the British Grand Prix, beating works Jaguars and Aston Martins to do so. In 1957 Scott-Brown dominated the British sports-car racing season winning 11 of the 14 races, this time in a Lister Jaguar. In 1958 orders were gained for an improved version which conformed to international regulations. Stirling Moss won the support race for the British Grand Prix and Lister Chevrolets dominated the American sports car season. Two cars were entered for the Le Mans 24 hour race, one finishing in 15th place. Lister Jaguar returned to Le Mans the next year, but without success, the lead car was running in fourth place when it was forced to retire. At the end of 1959, after 50 cars had been built, the general engineering side of the Cambridge business finally squeezed out car production. As well as Bristol, Jaguar and Chevrolet engines, versions from MG and Maserati had also been used. From 1959 to the early 1980s the Lister name was not seen in competitive racing.

In 1983 Laurence Pearce acquired the Lister name and restarted production of Lister Jaguars in a new factory in Leatherhead. The cars were totally new and designed jointly by Pearce and Brian Lister for a series of races for Jaguar sports cars known as the Lister Challenge. Over the next decade 41 modified Jaguars were produced but Pearce wanted to construct a purpose-built 'front mid-engined ' supercar with a strong yet light integral body/chassis, outstanding dynamics and room for four people and their luggage. The answer was 'The Storm' which was introduced at the 1994 London Motor Show. By early 1995 five Storms had been delivered, priced at £187,000 plus taxes for the 'standard' model, with an extra £50,000 for the 800bhp version.

The Storm had a chassis of light aluminium sandwich; bonded and riveted carbon-fibre panels; and a Jaguar-based 7litre V-12 engine, force-fed by twin superchargers; a six-speed Getrag gearbox; race-derived double-wishbone front suspension and complex, five-link rear suspension and a flat bottom incorporating down-force 'tunnels'. This combination, producing 600 bhp, gives the car a top speed of 220mph and is faster than any other four-seat road car. All other super-cars are two seat with the exception of the McLaren F1 which has three.

A two-seat Storm has been rumoured for some time to be under development but has not yet been seen in public, in spite of a number of orders being taken it seems. The emergence of GT racing as the world's top sports car arena over the past few years has provided the ideal platform for Lister to return to international competition. Undoubtedly all available resources, including the all-important matter of funding, have gone into this. There were rumours in the nineties of Arab money being acquired, but none was made public. However for a number of years the cars ran under the black and white colours of Newcastle United football club through the sponsorship of Sir John Hall, then chairman of the club.

A Storm, driven by Julian Bailey and Tiff Needell, with an 800bhp 48-valve Jaguar engine, ran without success at Le Mans in 1995. The 'Daily Telegraph' reported "The Storm ran in the 1995 Le Mans 24 Hour Race, after originally only being accepted as a reserve. The car had not run competitively anywhere else before and had not had a 'proper' testing. The pit crew were all 'amateurs' in all senses of the word. The car ran well initially, lapping as fast as the McLarens, but sadly retired after 5 hours with engine trouble." Since then the Lister Storm has run in a further three Le Mans races, three Daytona 24 hours and selected races in the BPR International GT Series, always in a podium position in the last, the BRDC GT Championships, finishing second in 1998, the American sportscar racing series and the FIA Global GT Championship.

In 1999 the Storm won both classes of the BRDC GT Championships, with Julian Bailey and Jamie Campbell-Walker in the GT1 car, and David Warnock in the GT2 car. The former pair also won the RAC Tourist Trophy and the Oulton Park Gold Cup. The GT1 won seven of the eleven British rounds, Warnock winning all six races in which the GT2 car was entered. Thorkilld Thyrring won the Danish Grand Prix in a Storm and Peter Hardman and Nicolaus Springer came second in the final two races of the Spanish GT Championship.

The Lister Storm won the 2000 FIA Constructors' World Championship and Bailey and Campbell-Walker the Drivers' Championship winning 5 out of 10 races with 6 pole positions. They also won the British Empire Trophy at Silverstone, repeating Archie Scott-Brown's feat of fifty years ago.

For 2003 the new Storm LMP900 underwent rigorous testing before its first race in Sebring, Florida in March, remembering the under-preparation for the Storm's first race. It also ran again at Le Mans, competing in the top category against the all-conquering Audis. The car was also entered in a number of other events, including the FIA GT Championship again, aiming to repeat the success of 2000. Campbell-Walker was now the lead driver with Nathan Kinch, Andrea Piccini and Jean-Denis Delatraz in support.

Caterham, McLaren and Lister all in their different ways continue to uphold the name of the county in motor sport, following in the earlier tradition of Brabham, Cooper, Connaught and others.

John Barnard. Before moving on it is worth noting the presence of a major racing car designer in Surrey. John Barnard did not have an in-depth technical education unlike many of his contemporaries, but gained a Diploma from Watford College of Technology. His first job was industrial design work for GEC, in his spare time he tinkered with an Austin Healey Sprite with a souped-up engine.

In 1968 he joined Lola as a junior designer where one of his colleagues was Patrick Head, the two becoming firm friends. In 1972 he moved to McLaren and worked under Gordon Coppuck on the M16 Indycar, the M23 World Championship-winning

Formula 1 car and the Formula 5000 M25. In 1975 he was hired by Parnelli Jones to design a F1 car, but the American soon dropped the idea and Barnard designed the Parnelli VPJ6 Indycar for him instead. Barnard, working from home, then designed the Chaparral 2K with which Johnny Rutherford won the 1980 Indy 500 and the Indycar title.

Ron Dennis, then running the Project 4 team, asked Barnard to design a revolutionary GP car made entirely of composite materials. This became the MP4/1 which led to an entire family of successful F1 McLarens in the 1980s. Courted by Ferrari in 1987 Barnard was able to dictate his terms, he was given $2 million and his own design centre, Ferrari Guildford Technical Office. It was here that he masterminded his next technical breakthrough, the semi-automatic gearbox. He was then lured away by Benetton to set up the Benetton Advanced Research Group at Godalming and there designed the B191, which was the basis for the 1994 World Championship-winning B194. Benetton, now Renault, eventually moved their research and design facility to Oxford, nearer to their production unit.

Barnard fell out with Benetton over money and worked briefly on a Toyota project which never got off the ground. Ferrari wanted him back, offering him his own design office in Surrey as he was unwilling to move to Italy. So he rejoined the team at the Ferrari Design and Development Office at Shalford. At the end of 1997 Barnard bought the design centre from Ferrari and set up B3 Technologies, specialising in suspension, braking and steering systems. His first commission was with Arrows, but the deal turned sour in mid 1998 after a dispute over money – again – with Tom Walkinshaw who was concerned that B3 was also working with Prost Grand Prix. The dispute was settled and Barnard acted as technical consultant to Prost in 1999 while continuing to run B3 Technologies. Subsequently both Prost Grand Prix and Arrows withdrew from F1 racing due to financial problems. In 2000 there was a proposal to move into new premises on the site of the old Artington cold store site, but there was a protracted hold up until 'major issues concerning a client of the company' were resolved. Barnard decided to try motorcycle racing and at the beginning of 2003 became technical director of the Kenny Roberts MotoGP team.

References
The History of Motor Racing: William Boddy, 1978
The New Encyclopaedia of Motorcars: Ed. G N Georgano, 1982

British Car Factories from 1896: P Collins & M Stratton, 1993
HRG – The Sportman's Ideal: I Dussek, 1985
The Lotus & Caterham Sevens: J Coulter, 1988
Grand Prix Racing Web Site: 2003
Trojan Museum Trust Web Site: 2003
Mika Hakkinen, San Marino GP2000@ The Cahier Archive Web Site: 2003

Coach and Body Builders

There were two important car, bus and coach body builders in the county, and others of lesser importance, none of which has survived until the present. The two significant ones were E D Abbott in Farnham and Weymann in Addlestone.

E D ABBOTT, Farnham. 1928 to 1966. Coachbuilding started in Wrecclesham before the first world war at Warrens works near the Cricketers public house. In 1920 Page and Hunt Ltd. was established, run by the former, who had been a painter at Warrens, and financed by the latter, who was in business in Castle Street, Farnham. They moved to larger premises by the railway bordering Weydon Lane and in the twenties the firm specialised in custom-built bodies on Armstrong Siddeley and Daimler chassis but also used American models by Packard and La Salle, regularly exhibiting at Motor Shows during this period. The

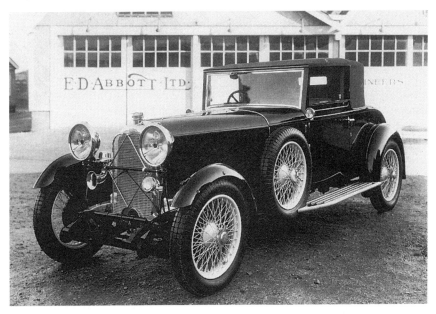

An Abbott-bodied Lagonda outside the works at Farnham in the mid-thirties *Museum of Farnham*

Two Bentleys and a Lanchester at Abbotts in the late thirties *Museum of Farnham*

recession hit the business badly and it went into liquidation in 1928. E D Abbott was the chief salesman and he bought the business from its owners and changed the name to his own.

To keep the workforce busy during this difficult period he extended operations to include work on commercial chassis and the refurbishing of older cars, including Rolls Royce, even building a series of vans on old Rolls chassis, much to the disapproval of that firm. Under Abbott the company prospered and in the thirties reverted again to building high quality coachwork on Rolls Royce, Daimler and Lagonda chassis, specialising in convertibles. This led to a contract with Rootes for a series of drophead bodies on the Talbot Ten, a similar contract being obtained from AFN of Isleworth, importers of BMW sports cars. (AFN are the initials of Archie Frazer Nash, the founder of the firm). The Abbott-built Type 45 BMW was generally thought not to look as good as the model imported with German-built Reutter bodies.

During the early hours of 30 December 1935 a disastrous fire broke out in the sawmill and spread quickly to the body shop. About 30 new cars, mainly Frazer Nash BMW and Talbot were destroyed. The damage was estimated at the time to have cost the firm some £20,000. Temporary buildings were quickly erected while the factory was rebuilt. About 110 employees were on the payroll at this time.

Some attractive individual bodies were built on Aston Martin and Atalanta chassis in the late thirties, but the bulk of business immediately before WW2 was the volume production of drophead coupé bodies for the small Daimler, for whom Abbotts also acted as local agents. During the thirties the firm had branched out into the manufacture of light aircraft and gliders, this coming about largely through the personal enthusiasm for flying by Abbott, who had been a pilot in WWI.

During WW2 the high grade skills of the workforce were used to make aircraft components and by the late forties the firm was back into its original business with a series of high-grade bodies on Rolls Royce, Bentley and Healey chassis. Some quite splendid bodies were built on Delahaye, Jaguar and Allard chassis at this time. By the late fifties the company was controlled by R G Sutherland, late of Aston Martin. He recognised that with more manufacturers turning to integral chassis and body construction there was little future in the traditional forms of coachbuilding.

So policy was changed and a major contract was negotiated with Ford to convert larger models from their range into estate cars, beginning in 1953 with the Mk. I Consuls, Zephyrs and Zodiacs. At the time it was not practicable to integrate the special

A Sunbeam Talbot in the Abbott workshops in the fifties *Chris Shepheard collection*

163

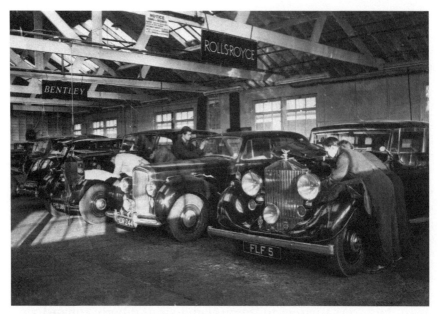

A Rolls Royce and a Bentley at Abbotts *Chris Shepheard collection*

estate bodies into the normal Ford production line, so complete cars were shipped down to Farnham where they were cut down and re-built as estate cars. As a final swan song to tradition a striking body was built on a Ferrari Type 212 chassis, the most expensive bodywork Abbott ever produced, it was invoiced at £8,888. The Ford estates were well received and the company expanded when other famous coachbuilders, such as Hooper, Gurney Nutting and H J Mulliner were shutting up shop. Estate car production continued on Marks II, III and the early Mark IV Zephyrs and Corsairs.

By 1966 it was evident that Abbotts lacked the facilities to expand sufficiently to be able to satisfy the increasing demand, so Ford took back the business and integrated the estate body production into their car assembly lines. Abbotts had no other business to fall back on or to develop so the firm went into liquidation. The buildings remained empty for a number of years before being converted into a small industrial estate. Virtually nothing now remains of the original buildings, the showroom was occupied by a tile warehouse until the early nineties and the north workshops by a carpet showroom. The south workshops, which had been the last of the post WWI buildings to survive, were finally demolished in 1980 and the site redeveloped.

WEYMANN, London and Addlestone. 1923 to 1966. Charles Terres Weymann was born of an American father and a French mother in Haiti in 1889. He lived in Paris and experimented before WWI with aircraft design and became a successful pilot, serving in the French Air Force during the war. In 1921 he produced a car built on aircraft principles with a flexible wooden frame and fabric covering. There were steel joints in the frame so that wood never rubbed against wood, which lead to a 'cracking' noise as the car moved.

In 1923 he opened a factory in north-west London to manufacture car fittings and instruments as well as the fabric-covered car bodies. In 1925 he formed Weymann's Motor Bodies (1925) Ltd. and moved into the former premises of the Cunard Motor & Carriage Co. Ltd. in Putney. He also opened an American factory in Indianapolis in 1926 to build fabric bodies for Stutz cars, but they proved unsuitable for the higher speeds now being achieved on the still poor rural roads in the US. So the American business soon closed whilst the British demand was also now for metal bodies, albeit still for a time on wooden chassis, but soon all-metal integrated chassis and bodies became the norm except for such idiosyncrasies as the Morgan, which to this day has hand-beaten aluminium bodies on an ash frame.

In 1928 Weymann moved to the old Bleriot factory at Addlestone, which had been erected in 1916 to build SPAD fighters. Post war it had been used by the Air Navigation & Engineering Co. who built the Bleriot Whippet and Eric Longden light cars. Car bodies were built at first by Weymann to individual order and then in batches, but were never mass-

Weymann fabric body on a 1926 Stutz *Francis Haveron collection*

produced. Riley was the biggest customer, the 'Monaco' and 'Biarritz' on Riley 9 chassis were the most popular. Fabric body production ceased in 1932. Meanwhile the building of bus bodies had started in 1929 when seven were made, ten years later output was nearly 1,000. Weymann resigned from the board, not prepared to accept the radical change in policy and moved back to France to look after that side of the firm. He died in 1976, reportedly in comparative poverty. E G Izod and R A Homfray-Davis became joint Managing Directors, the latter had become Chairman by 1939.

The first bus bodies had a wooden frame with metal panels. New all-metal bodies, influenced by Metropolitan-Cammell designs were introduced by Arthur Froggat who had joined the firm as General Manager. During the thirties the building of bus bodies expanded, mainly for London Transport but also in more limited numbers for other customers. Ambulances, lorry cabs and prison vans were also built at this time, but the firm realised that they could not compete with the other larger specialists so never took up the production of all-metal car bodies. They produced their first double-decked bus in 1930 and in 1932 an agreement was reached with Metropolitan-Cammell to create a joint sales company, Metropolitan-Cammell Weymann. Work obtained through this joint arrangement was allocated on a 60–40 percentage basis between Birmingham and Addlestone.

During WWII no private buses were completed but some 1,500 military buses were built as well as 8,800 assorted military vehicles including tank transporters, radio vans and armoured vehicles. After the war there was a huge demand for buses, production at Addlestone peaking in 1949 when 972 were built by a workforce then at a peak of 1,500. The most popular was the RT3 of which some 2,400 were supplied to London Transport between 1945 and 1953. This was a double-decker built in collaboration with Park Royal, all parts being interchangeable to facilitate repairs and maintenance. By 1954 demand was tailing off resulting in the closure of 'J' shop which had been erected especially to build the RT3.

Demand for the RF single-decker, built for Green Line, also dropped adding to the firm's problems. A chassis-less single deck bus, the 'Olympic' was developed, 800 being built by 1953, and over 1,000 by 1957. This was the first of its type to be built in quantity anywhere. A development was the 'Olympian', and the 'Orion', a chassis-less double-decker weighing less than two tons had appeared in 1952. Numbers of these were supplied to South

Africa and an assembly plant was opened in Port Elizabeth to build the bus from kits supplied from Addlestone.

By 1960 production was down to 489 bus bodies of all types, almost half that of 1949. Attempts had been made to diversify, between 1952 and 1956 some 525 vehicle bodies had been built for the Ministry of Supply and between 1958 and 1965 some 390 taxi bodies were made for Beardmore. The Prudential Insurance Co. had been buying into Weymann over the years, having seen it as a promising investment, but then decided to sell their shares to a shipping company, United Molasses Co. They in turn had continued to buy into the company and in 1946 had taken over control. As post-war demand from London Transport in particular declined, Leyland took over AEC, who owned Park Royal, direct competitors of Weymann. Work previously shared on the RT3 was now going entirely to Park Royal, as all London buses were traditionally supplied by AEC, the chassis and engines by themselves and now all bodies by Park Royal.

In 1961 only 289 bus bodies were produced, partly due to the recession, but also due to a serious fire. Two wooden boats were being constructed during a particularly slack period and pitch, which was used to seal the joints, boiled over and burst into flames. Much machinery was damaged as were a number of part-finished buses. Damage was initially estimated at £500,000, subsequently revised to nearer £100,000. A temporary replacement building was erected which lasted through to the end. In February 1964 a damaging strike occurred in the Finishing Department, involving 85 workers and lasted 21 weeks. The cause was the inclusion of two long-serving trade union officials in a list of 13 redundancies. One had 27 year's service, the other 23. As a result 200 men were laid off and a further 160 left the firm. Relations between management and the National Union of Vehicle Builders, who had been active in the factory since 1936, were at a low point. It was suggested that management was taking the opportunity to rid themselves of known trouble-makers.

A committee under A J Scamp, Personnel Director of GEC, finally arrived at conditions acceptable to both sides for a resumption of work. The two union officials were offered re-employment, provided that they held no union office for three years. Business continued to decline, between 1961 and 1964 output was down to under ten vehicles per week. After the strike they fell further to seven buses a week, an insufficient level to sustain the business. The press announced on 25 June 1965 that

167

the factory was to close, to be effective early in 1966. It was also disclosed that the business had been sold to Metropolitan-Cammell some two years previously.

By June 1965 there were 550 employees left and 400 of them sought to buy out the business from Metropolitan-Cammell, who had by then put the property up for sale. Their plans came to nothing, for they were unable to raise the capital and neither were Metropolitan-Cammell particularly helpful either. In January 1966 the site was bought by Brixton Estates and the factory closed down on 31 March that year. In September most of the site was leased to Plessey for 99 years, but J Caddy (Coachbuilders) Ltd. took out a 27 year lease on the 'new' paint shop, which had been built in 1947. But in May 1969 Caddy moved out to a site in Worcestershire and Plessey bought up their lease. By 1989, following a series of take-overs and mergers in the electronics industry the Addlestone factory carried the Marconi name over the door.

During the period from 1929 to 1966 a total of 23,745 vehicle bodies were produced by Weymanns at Addlestone. This included 15,104 bus bodies, 337 cars, 65 ambulances, 334 lorry cabs, 102 lorries, 19 prison vans and 9,394 assorted vehicles for the Ministry of Supply. The balance went to individual private customers.

Horse-drawn coach builders and motor garages turned their hand to building car bodies during the first quarter of the twentieth century. Before the days of mass production it was the normal thing to buy the chassis and engine from the manufacturer and have your own body fitted. It is impossible to try to record them all, a few of the more significant body-builders are included together with others that I have come across references to.

Two small bus body builders in the immediate post WWII period were DUTFIELD MOTORS and KING & TAYLOR, both of Godalming. Dutfield largely built on the Tilling Stevens K6LA7 chassis whilst King & Taylor specialised in smaller vehicles including the rare passenger version of the post-war Vulcan. In Leatherhead the firm of VENTHAM in Bridge Street (they also had a business in Dorking) ventured for a short time into building car bodies. They were famous in London in the 1830s as coachbuilders, moving to Leatherhead in the 1840s, where among other products London to Brighton stage coaches were built. After WWI they turned increasingly to motor body manufacture and repair, by 1929 it was virtually their sole

168

business. The firm closed in 1936 on the retirement of the grandson of the founder. The site was then let as a general engineering and garage business until 1985 when the site was cleared and redeveloped. A tyring platform from the coachbuilding era, though not from Venthams, and a hand-operated petrol pump from the garage on the site are now in the Leatherhead Museum.

Two Redhill firms of note were MEIR & SON and CHALMERS. The former were founded in 1863, building their first car body in 1901. By 1912 they claimed to have built some 500 bodies on a dozen different chassis, from Ariel to Vauxhall. That year they unveiled their contribution to a fad of the time, transformable coachwork. Their 'Nutshell' on a 3,308c Itala chassis was a four-seat tourer whose rear could be folded to create a two-seater with a 'fish tail' rear. Chalmers made their first GPO delivery van body in 1905, gun carriages during WWI and later converted cars into ambulances. In the 1930s they rebuilt Birkin's famous Le Mans winning Bentley. The firm closed during the 1950s.

A P COMPTON & Co. Ltd. and the ARROW COACHWORKS Ltd. were in Wimbledon during the 1920s, owned by Chota McGuffie. (See the Arab car, Appendix I).

References.
Local Transport – The E D Abbott Story: Richard Aspden and Chris Shepheard, Farnham Museum, 1985
Air–Road–Sea Addlestone: J H Rowe, 1992
The Weymann Story, Part 1; 1923–1945: John Senior, Alan Townsin and John Banks, 2002

Appendix I

Car and Commercial Vehicle Manufacturers

I have been able to trace over 120 different car, bus and commercial vehicle builders in the county. If they were in Surrey at the time they were in business I have included them, ignoring the present county boundaries. The list grows almost daily, I cannot guarantee that it is complete but is the most comprehensive I can come up with at the time of writing. Many builders, particularly in the early days, were general engineers, cycle makers or car distributors who turned their hand to manufacturing. A number, particularly builders of the short-lived light 'cycle-car' either side of the first world war, made but one or two experimental cars and records of these are sparse. My sources have been many and varied, including the lists prepared by Francis Haveron, after his correspondence with a number of people, including myself. But a number that were previously unknown to me I have identified through that monumental reference work, 'The New Encyclopaedia of Motorcars – 1885 to the present', edited by G N Georgano.

ABC: ABC Motors, Hersham 1920–1929. One of the longest-lived post WWI light cars, owing its relative success to the fact

ABC Regent, Lands End trial car 1921 *National Motor Museum*

that it retained and improved upon the sporting characteristics of the cycle-car and did not try to copy the heavier, if more comfortable, small family car. It had a 24hp air-cooled flat twin engine of 1203cc. It handled well with a top speed of 60mph. Some 8,000 cars were made. To the end both an electric starter and four-wheel brakes were extras. ABC made motor-cycle engines at Brooklands from 1912–1914, and at Hersham after moving there in 1914. In 1917 they built the infamous 'Dragonfly' aero engine, which proved to be completely unreliable after some 1,000 had been built towards a government order for 11,000. Thereafter the firm made more aero engines and auxiliary engines for aircraft until 1951 when the factory closed following a merger with Vickers Aircraft.

AC: AC Cars, Thames Ditton 1908–1976, Glasgow, Knebworth, Brooklands, Frimley, Camberley 1976 to date. (See Chapter Ten).

ACCUMULATOR INDUSTRIES: Accumulator Industries, Woking 1902–1903. This company made a heavy electric coach as well as a number of light electric two-seat cars, generally similar to the American Riker and Columbia. They had solid tyres and two 2.5hp Lundell motors

ALLARD: Allard, Leatherhead, late 1940s. Allard produced distinctive sports cars in Putney from 1937 to 1945, and in Clapham from 1945 to 1962. For a short time the company had an experimental and development shop for the J2 model in the Kingston Road behind Thorne's garage, which later became Pages, and is now a Shell service station.

ALTA: Alta Car and Engineering Co., Kingston upon Thames 1931–1954. (See Chapter Eleven).

ALTAIR: Altair Engineering, Reigate 2000 to date. A low-cost sports kit car developed by former Caterham engineer Tony Weale, weighing only 950 lbs due to the extensive use of light aluminium panelling. The car uses mainly Ford components.

ARGSON: Stanley Engineering, Egham 1923–1926. A three-wheeled petrol-engined single cylinder car with open seats and controlled by rotary steering.

171

An Atalanta in the 1939 Scottish Rally *National Motor Museum*

ATALANTA: Atalanta Motors Ltd., Staines 1937–1939. The first models had Gough designed four cylinder engines of 1.5 and 2 litre capacity developing 78 and 98 bhp which could be increased using an Arnott supercharger. In 1938 a model was offered with an American Lincoln V-12 engine of 4.3 litres. Two door saloon and drophead coupé bodies were available and a sports car with either cycle-type wings or running boards. The company disappeared with the outbreak of war.

AUTOTRIX: Edmunds and Wadden, Weybridge 1911–1914. A three-wheeler with either a 4hp JAP engine and belt drive, or a 9hp JAP engine, Chater-Lea gearbox and chain drive. (See Simplic).

AVERIES: Averies-Ponette Ltd., Englefield Green 1911–1915. John Averies imported the French Ponette car and in 1913 produced his own version based on a design by Paul Dupressoir and built in Maubeuge, France.

BABY BLAKE: E G Blake & Co., Croydon 1922. A cycle-car with a 2 stroke engine with infinitely variable drive. Only a few were built.

172

BAT: BAT Motor Manufacturing Co. Penge 1904–1909. A tri-car with enclosed wooden body for the passenger who sat in the front with the driver on a chair-like seat behind.

BEACON: Beacon Hill Motor Works, Hindhead 1912–1913. Beacon Motors Ltd. Liphook 1913–1914. A cycle-car with a cane body as an alternative to the usual coachbuilt one. The engine was a Griffon air-cooled V-twin with shaft drive to a 3-speed gearbox mounted on the rear axle.

BENTALL: Bentalls, Kingston and Maldon, Essex 1906–1913. Designed by L E Rowan Bentall, an agricultural engineer in Essex and brother of the founder of the store. The car, which was sold exclusively by the Kingston store, had a 4-cylinder 2,418cc engine and a standard 5 seat touring body by Munions of Chelmsford and cost £400. Some 100 cars were built, one is rumoured still to exist.

BERLIET: Berliet, Richmond. I have found no written record of this French car being built in Surrey, only a verbal reference obtained indirectly from a descendant of the Berliet family that cars were assembled in a building which was subsequently converted into the ice rink. This building is no longer with us.

BLAKE: F C Blake & Co. Kew (1901–1903). The firm was originally in Hammersmith in 1900, moving out to Kew a year later. They manufactured engines for other car builders also building a small number of complete cars themselves, including a 7hp 4-cylinder model as well as one with a 4hp single horizontal cylinder. After 1903 the firm concentrated on building light railway locomotives and marine engines.

BLERIOT-WHIPPET: Air Navigation & Engineering Co. Ltd. Addlestone (1920–1927). This light cyclecar was unique in that it had an infinitely variable transmission by pulley and belt, similar to the much later Dutch DAF The engine was a V-twin aircooled unit by Blackburne of Bookham. The Whippet was advertised in 1922 at £125 including dynamo lighting and spare wheel, and gave 'large car comfort for a small car price'. In 1922 a development was introduced with an 8.9hp engine, chain drive and reverse gear. A year later shaft drive and a conventional gearbox was fitted. It was one of the more successful and long-lived cyclecars of the period.

Advertisement for 1922 Bleriot Whippet *Chertsey Museum*

BOW-V-CAR:. The Plycar Co. Ltd. Upper Norwood 1922. Luton 1923. The car had a unitary body and chassis fitted with a 10hp V-twin 'Precision' engine with chain final drive. It was steered by a lever by the side of the driver's seat.

BRABHAM: Motor Racing Developments Ltd. Chessington (1962–1989). Milton Keynes (1990–1992). (See Chapter Eleven).

BRADBURY: Bradbury Bros. Croydon (1901–1902). They were agents for Pinart engines and made a few voiturettes, the French term for light cars, with 4.5hp single cylinder front-mounted engines and chain drive.

BRITISH SALMSON: British Salmson Aero Engines Ltd. Raynes Park (1934–1939). The first cars were 1.5 litre 4-cylinder twin ohc fast tourers based on the French Salmson S4C. In 1936 an entirely new British sports model was introduced with a 2.6 litre ohv engine and was built in very small numbers. By 1939 this was the only model offered, other than imported French built 4-cylinder cars.

BROTHERHOOD: Brotherhood-Crocker Motors Ltd. West Norwood (1904–1906). The car was designed by Percy Richardson, late of Daimler, and the engine was made by the London engineers, Peter Brotherhood. The first model was a 12/16hp 4-cylinder with double chain drive. Later, 20 and 40hp models were introduced, also with 4-cylinder engines. A member of the board, Lord Fitzwilliam a Yorkshire landowner, moved production to a new factory in Sheffield after the name was changed to Sheffield-Simplex and a few cars under that name built in West Norwood.

CARLETTE: Holstein Garage, Weybridge (1913). This cyclecar used an 8hp JAP V-twin engine taken to a countershaft by a belt. The shaft could be swung to and fro to give a variable gear. Final drive was to one rear wheel only. The car was reputed, when tuned, to be capable of 60mph.

CATERHAM: Caterham Cars, Caterham and Crayford, Kent (1973 to date). (See Chapter Eleven).

CFB: Car Syndicate Ltd. Upper Norwood. (1920–1921). A light car with an 8hp air-cooled V-twin engine and a complicated transmission system involving a friction disc driving a countershaft on which were mounted two pulleys from which the drive was taken to the rear wheels by rubber belts.

CHRYSLER: Chrysler Ltd. Kew (1928–1960). The American company set up an assembly plant to build cars from imported kits in 1928 on the site of Maxwell cars who had imported Chryslers following the take-over by that company of the

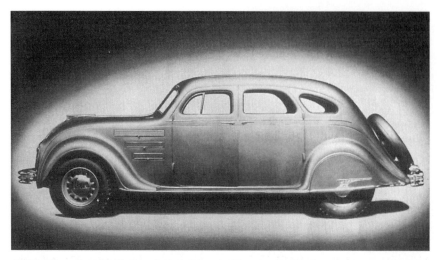

1934 Chrysler Airflow saloon *Francis Haveron collection*

Maxwell Motor Corporation of Detroit in 1923. The 1934 Airflow was ahead of its time with a streamlined body and a large, powerful, and efficient engine. Chrysler engines were used by several British sports car manufacturers in the thirties, forties and fifties.

COLLINDA: Ashtead (2000 to date). This is a small solar-powered electric rickshaw developed by a chemical distributor. It can either be powered direct from the solar panels to the electric motor or via storage batteries. In good solar conditions it can produce 5hp giving good acceleration and a speed of 30kmh with a range of 100 miles a day. It is intended to replace cycle and motor rickshaws in India and the Far East.

COMET: Comet Car & Manufacturing Co. Croydon (1935–1937). Not to be confused with the Comet car produced in 1921 by the Preston Autocar Co. in London. The Croydon Comet was a high performance light car which never progressed beyond the prototype stage. It had a 1.2 litre 4-cylinder ohv engine developing 46bhp, a 4-speed gearbox, and independent front suspension. It was proposed to offer two and four seater sportscars and saloons and drophead coupés, with bodies by Abbott, with prices from £435 to £465.

CONDOR: The Condor Motorcar Co. Guildford (1960). The first, and only production specification of this unsuccessful

176

Formula Junior racing car featured a front-mounted Triumph Herald engine and gearbox, BMC differential, inboard rear brakes and a square-sectioned tubular space-frame fitted with an aluminium body. Condor wheels subsequently became popular with other car manufacturers.

CONNAUGHT: Continental Cars Ltd. Send (1949–1951), Connaught Engineering Send (1951–1957). (See Chapter Eleven).

COOPER: Cooper Car Co. Surbiton (1948–1965), Byfleet (1965–1972). (See Chapter Eleven).

COWEY: Cowey Engineering Co. Kew Gardens (1913–1915). The company speciality was a pneumatic suspension system whereby the car was carried on four cylinders of compressed air. It incorporated automatic levelling, as on the Citroën DS19 which was hailed as a breakthrough when it appeared in the nineteen-forties.

CRAIG DÖRWALD (AILSA CRAIG): Putney Motor Co. Putney (1902–1912). Cars were usually made to special order and to individual design. A 5 hp single-cylinder single-speed car was built in 1902 followed by a 10 hp 2-cylinder commercial traveller's car in 1903. Later 'standard' models were 8 hp, 18 hp and 36 hp, while the largest car built was a 50 hp 4-cylinder, with a barouche body by Hamshaw, for the Earl of Norbury. Only 12 cars were made in total, the firm was more famous for its marine engines, making the world's first V-12 of 150 hp in 1904.

CRAYSHAW WILLIAMS: Crayshaw Williams Ltd. Ashtead (1904–1906). This company made two models of a 4-cylinder car, with 14/16 and 20/24hp Simms engines. They used chain drive and in appearance resembled a Mercedes.

DENNIS: Dennis Bros. (1899–1901), Dennis Bros. Ltd. (1901–1913 and 1918–1972), Dennis Bros. 1913 Ltd. (1913–1918), Dennis Motors Ltd. (1972–1973), Hestair Dennis (1973–1984), Dennis Specialist Vehicles (1984–2000), Transbus Dennis (2000–to date). (See Chapter Ten).

DEREK: Derek Motors Ltd. West Norwood (1925–1926). A conventional light car with 9/20hp side valve or 10/28hp ohv Chapius-Dornier engines. Two or four seat open bodies were offered.

DE SOTO: Kew (1928–1960). During the thirties Chrysler introduced more up market versions of their imported US kit cars badged De Soto. They were assembled at Kew.

DODGE: Kew (1928–1960). US Dodge trucks were assembled at the Chrysler plant during the late thirties and forties from imported kits. (Dodge had been taken over by Chrysler in the twenties). They were not wholly successful due to the iniquities of the British taxation system.

DURANT: Farnham (1894). (See Chapter Five).

EAGLET: Silent Transport Ltd. Woking (1948). Introduced when there was no basic petrol ration, the Eaglet was a light electric 3-wheeled coupé with a range of 30 miles per charge, and a speed of 30mph. It was expensive for the time at £412, the makers had a more fruitful, if short-lived, business converting Opel Cadets and Fiat Topolinos to electric power.

ELVA: Elva Engineering, Bexhill (1958–1961), Trojan Ltd. Croydon (1962–1965), Sheppard Customised Sports Cars Ltd. (Shenley) 1965–1969. The first Elva was a low-cost sports racing car designed by Frank Nichols in 1955. It appeared as the Courier in a road version, for export only, in 1958. Cars and kits for the home market did not appear until 1960. The car had many proprietary components including an MG A engine and Riley back axle. After 400 cars had been built production ceased for nine months before restarting at the Trojan works. Trojan built the MkIII and MkIV versions with front disc brakes, with rear ones fitted later to the MkIV. Optional engines were the Ford Cortina GT and the 1.8 litre MG B. In 1963 the MkVII was introduced with a 1588cc Ford engine and an elegant body designed by Fiore and made by Fissore of Turin. In 1964 Trojan took over the business completely and continued building the Elva until the first McLaren cars went into production under the McLaren-Elva name. Transfer to Shenley in 1965 led to a gradual run-down of the Elva business and name.

EMERALD: Douglas Cox & Co. West Norwood (1903–1904). This was a light two-seat voiturette with a 4 hp single-cylinder engine, a 2-speed gearbox and belt drive to the rear axle. Cox later bought the Weller works, also in West Norwood, where he built the Osterfield car (qv).

EMERYSON: Twickenham (1949–1952), Send (1960–1961). The first car was a 500cc racing car with front-wheel drive and independent rubber suspension, giving the car the ability to corner rapidly. Only eight cars were built and successes were few. In 1952 the weight was reduced and coil suspension fitted. In 1961, in conjunction with Connaught, a few Formula Junior cars were built in the Connaught works at Send. Design was conventional as was a team of Maserati-engined Formula 1 cars that were built for the Equipe Nationale Belge. They had an erratic career, later re-emerging as the US sponsored Sciroccos.

ERIC-LONGDON: Air Navigation & Engineering Co. Addlestone (1922–1927). This car was built by the same company that took over production of the Bleriot Whippett. It had either an 8hp side valve, or 10hp OHV V-twin JAP engine, the latter reputably giving the car a maximum speed of over 70mph. The cars had shaft drive and polished aluminium bodies. Two 4-cylinder models were shown at the 1922 Olympia Motor Show, with either 9hp Alpha or 11hp Coventry Simplex engines.

FASTRAX: Brown and Root Ltd. Leatherhead (2001 to date). The British base of the American engineering group obtained a 20 year licence to build these US designed heavy equipment, i.e. tank transporters, for the Ministry of Defence. They will ultimately replace the Army's existing Antar fleet.

FELDAY: Felday Engineering Ltd. Dorking (1962–1966). Peter Westbury produced one-off 4-wheel drive Daimler V-8 powered cars which achieved hill-climb successes including, in 1963 and 1964, the British Hill-Climb Championship. A 2-wheel drive version was then offered to the public, fitted with a 4.7 litre rear-mounted Ford engine driving through a Hewland gearbox.

FIREFLY: Firefly Motor & Engineering Co. Ltd. Croydon (1902–1904). Initially these were shaft-driven light cars powered by 6hp Aster or de Dion engines. For 1903 these were replaced by chain-driven cars with 9 or 12hp Herald 2-cylinder engines.

FORSTER: Forster Light Cars Ltd. Richmond (1922). One of the less successful light cars of the twenties. It used a 10hp 2-cylinder engine and cost £225, but progressed little beyond the prototype stage.

FRAZER NASH: Frazer Nash Ltd. Kingston (1924–1926), Isleworth (1926–1957). Capt. Archie Frazer Nash left GN Ltd., the company he had helped set up, to form his own business. At first he made orthodox family cars with shaft drive and water-cooled 4-cylinder engines based on the Deemster. He soon reverted to type however with a new car, developed from the GN, retaining its dog-clutch gear change, separate chains for each of the three forward speeds and high ratio steering. He adopted the side-valve water-cooled 4-cylinder 1.5 litre Anzani engine which gave 40bhp. With the Aston Martin, the Frazer Nash was Britain's nearest answer to the Bugatti and Alfa Romeo, the true sports cars of the period.

The car was so popular that it remained in production, basically unchanged, for 15 years, even though dog-clutches and chain drive were outmoded even when it was introduced. The last true Frazer-Nash was made in 1939, production from then, until the firm withdrew from car manufacture in 1957, was a model based on, and produced jointly with, BMW. The marque was taken over by Bristol who are still in business today, the cars albeit now fitted with large American engines.

GENERAL: General Motor Car Co. Norbury (1902–1903), Mitcham (1903–1905). The company was supposed to be building a 24hp racing car for the 1902 Bexhill Speed Trials, but it never appeared. However at the end of 1902 a racer was made with a 40hp Buchet engine. In 1903 more practical cars were made with 6.5hp Aster or 12hp Buchet engines. The 1904 car had a spiral radiator and shaft drive. In 1905, shortly before the demise of the marque, larger cars were built with 30hp Simms and 40hp Buchet engines.

GODFREY PROCTOR: Godfrey Proctor Richmond (1928–1929). A light sports car based on the Austin Seven with improvements to the engine and suspension. Bodywork was by Newns of Thames Ditton. Only ten cars were built.

GRAHAM HILL: Graham Hill Cars Byfleet (1975). Graham Hill retired from Grand Prix driving in 1975 and set up his own company to develop Formula 1 and sports cars. It never actually produced any cars before his untimely death in an air crash at the end of the year and the firm closed down.

GUILDFORD: Griffith Engineering Works, Guildford (1920).
This was a cyclecar with a Blackburne 8hp V-twin engine and chain drive. The makers stated that they were willing to sell the design to anyone willing to manufacture it in quantity. Apparently there were no takers, so the car never went into production or was put on the market.

HENRY: Oxted Motor Co. (1920). Designed by Geoffrey Henry using US manufactured components. Development cars were thought to have been built in the US but it never went into full-scale production.

HRG: HRG Engineering Co. Ltd. Tolworth (1936–1956). (See Chapter Eleven).

HORLEY: Horley Motor and Engineering Co. (1904–1907).
One of the first companies to achieve the magic price of 100gns for a complete car. This was a light shaft-driven two-seater with an 8hp single cylinder MMC engine originally marketed as the 'No-Name'. In 1906 the engine was uprated to 9hp and in 1907 replaced by an 8.5hp White & Poppe engine when the price went over the 100 gns. mark.

HOWARD: Howard Motor Works Sutton (1913). A limited production cyclecar with an 8hp JAP engine, friction transmission and roller chain final drive.

HP: Hilton-Pearcy Motors Woking (1926–1928). This was the last of the cyclecars, a simple 3-wheeler with a 500cc JAP engine, chain drive to a 3-speed Sturmey-Archer gearbox and final drive also by chain to the rear wheel. A modified 344cc JAP engined version took 18 Class H records at Brooklands. The price was only £65, less than half that for the Austin Seven, but the latter gave buyers more comfort. Only 40 HPs were made.

HWM: H W Motors Ltd. Walton-on-Thames (1950–1956). (See Chapter Eleven).

HUMMING-BIRD: Pippbrook Garage, Dorking (1948–1950).
This was not a new-build car in any sense. but was the name given to pre-war Austin Sevens, refurbished and sold by the Pippbrook Garage to meet an insatiable demand for cars – any cars – after WWII.

HUTTON: J E Hutton Ltd, Northallerton, Yorks. (1900–1902), Thames Ditton (1903–1905), Napier & Sons Ltd. Acton (1908).
Also known as the Simplex, the first Hutton was a Voiturette, but the Thames Ditton cars were conventional machines with a 4-cylinder engine of either 12 or 20hp, and shaft drive. An experimental car was made with Barber automatic transmission, but was not put into production. The final phase of the Hutton came in 1908 when three 4-cylinder cars were made in the Napier factory under the Hutton name because S F Edge, later to be involved with AC Cars at Thames Ditton, had decried the 4-cylinder engine so much that he refused them to run under the Napier name. However the Hutton driven by W Watson won the TT Race and the car still exists to this day.

IMPERIAL: The Anti-Vibrator Co. Ltd.. Croydon (1904–1905).
Not to be confused with car companies of the same name in both London and Manchester, and two in the US, all before the first World War. This car was an electric-powered landaulet with two 3hp motors mounted in the rear wheels. It was unusual for its time in having an integral body/chassis construction.

INVICTA: Invicta Cars Cobham (1925–1933), Chelsea (1933–1938), Virginia Water (1946–1950). In 1925 Noel Macklin, who had been associated with the Eric-Campbell and Silver Hawk cars, and Oliver Lyle of the sugar family, introduced a new type of car to the British market, an assembly factory having been set up in the back garden of Macklin's home at Fairmile Cottage in Cobham. The concept was to combine in an assembled car the American attributes of flexibility and performance with British quality and road holding. The Meadows 2.5 litre, 6-cylinder engine was chosen, it had push-rod overhead valves and its low torque characteristics permitted acceleration from walking pace to 60mph in top gear, although a 4-speed gearbox was fitted. The car was demonstrated by being driven up Guildford High Street in top gear from virtually a standing start. The cars sustained high-speed cruising and reliability and became legendary after winning the Dewar Trophy in 1928 and 1929. The car had a row of distinctive rivets down the bonnet, reminiscent of a Rolls Royce, its only poor features were the brakes. In 1926 a 3litre engine was offered and in 1929 a 4.5 litre, which became standard in 1930. The car was always expensive and in 1932 a smaller model was introduced in an attempt to stave off pending financial disaster. This car had a

Donald Healey and F M Montgomery in Poland in their 4.5 litre Invicta during the 1933 Monte Carlo rally *National Motor Museum*

1929 4.5 Invicta at Modena, 2004 *Peter Tarplee collection*

1.5 litre Blackburne 6-cylinder engine. It gave the same famed flexibility, but not the performance, and only ahandful were made. Both models had the Wilson self-changing gearbox. Whilst Macklin went on to make the Railton, the Invicta name was sold on in 1933, and when in 1935 production ceased only around 1,000 cars had been made at both Cobham and Chelsea.

In 1946 the name was briefly revived at Virginia Water with a 3litre, 6-cylinder Meadows-engined luxury car called the 'Black Prince'. It was horribly expensive and only 20 were made. On the collapse of the company the assets were acquired by AFN Ltd., the manufacturers of the Frazer Nash. The name has reappeared again in the twenty-first century, having being bought by a west-country entrepreneur who has launched a hand-built high speed sports-racer, only a handful have been so far been made.

ITALA: Itala Cars Brooklands (1912–1915). Itala of Turin started making cars in 1904, similar in appearance to the Mercedes of the period. By 1908 an extensive range of models was offered from a 2.6 litre 4-cylinder car up to monster 11.1 and 12.9 litre 6-cylinder engined cars, which became successful racers. The 12.9 litre cost £1,600 as a chassis in England, prompting the firm to open up an assembly plant at the new Brooklands racing track. Supplies became difficult at the outbreak of war in 1914, racing ceased at Brooklands for the duration and the demand for large cars was limited. In 1915 the plant was bought by Vickers who then undertook the building of military aircraft there and formed the base from which the inter-war years major aircraft assembly factory was developed.

JAG: JAG Cars Thames Ditton (1950–1952), RGS Automotive Components, Windsor (1954–1956). The first JAG, built by John Griffiths, had a Ford V-8 2,633 cc engine and a stark 2 seat open body. Later the car was fitted with either a Ford 1,172 cc or MG 1,800 cc engine, achieving some competition success. It was also available as a 'kit car' for home construction. Only some fifty cars were made.

JAPPIC: Jarvis & Sons Wimbledon (1925). This was a chain-driven single-seat cyclecar with quarter-eliptic suspension. It was offered with either a 350 or 500cc JAP engine.

JBM: James Boothby Motors Ltd, Horley and Crawley (1947–1950). A very light two-seater, with an excessively long wheelbase, powered by a modified Ford engine giving 120bhp. The cars were assembled from re-conditioned components, the price was £750.

JOHNSTON: Johnston Sweepers Ltd. Dorking (1924 to date). The company manufactures municipal and contractor cleansing vehicles mounted on proprietary engines and chassis. The current range is from 4 tons to over 20 tons gross vehicle weight. The 600 series has an auxiliary Perkins 4004.42 diesel engine powering the suction impeller fan, hydraulic, water and electrical systems and is working in more than 80 countries for over 1,000 customers.

KNIGHT: Farnham. Pioneering experimental steam car 1868, petrol-engined vehicle 1895. (See Chapter Five).

LAD: Oakleigh Motor Co. West Dulwich (1913–1914), LAD Productions Ltd. Farnham (1923–1926). One of the simplest and lightest cyclecars. Sold basically as a single-seater, two-seater versions were made to special order. The car had a pointed nose and a completely exposed 5.5 hp single-cylinder Stag engine at the rear, driving the rear axle via a chain. Only one speed was fitted and steering was by wire and bobbin. The price was £60. The Farnham-built cars were 3-wheeled single-seaters with either a 2.75 hp Blackburne or 3.5 hp Precision side mounted engine.

LAGONDA: Staines (1906–1947), Feltham (1947–1962), Aston-Martin Lagonda Newport Pagnell (1961 to date). Although the postal address was Staines, the factory was in fact in Egham. The founder was an American, William Gunn, who came over to England in 1897 and made motorcycles and boats in his garden. He built and opened his factory in 1906 to build both light and heavy touring cars. Lagonda is American Indian for 'Blue Creek', Gunn's home town. In 1910 a Lagonda won the St. Petersburg Rally and the car was bought by the Tsar. Between 1920 and 1939 fine 3 and 4 litre sports cars were made, winning at Le Mans in 1935. A 1.5 litre, less refined model was given the name Rapier, these were never built at Egham, but in a new factory in Feltham. The 1928 3 litre 6-cylinder ohv engine designed by Arthur Davidson had virtually silent running between 300,000 miles overhauls and was probably the best Lagonda produced. In 1947 the company was bought by David

Inside the Lagonda factory c1930 *Egham Museum*

Brown and a luxurious model was built at Feltham, using the 4 litre Aston Martin engine. Subsequently the joint firm moved to Newport Pagnell when the Lagonda name was dropped only to be briefly revived when Ford bought up the business. The Egham site was sold to Petters, diesel engine manufacturers, they eventually closed down and the site was redeveloped in 1989.

LEYLAND: Kingston (1920–1951). In 1920 Leyland Motors took out a long lease on the No 1 Aircraft Factory site in Richmond Road, Ham from Sopwith Aviation to rebuild over 3000 of their 6000 lorries sold to the War Department and the RAF during WWI. They wanted to ensure that the vehicles were in good condition before putting them onto the second-hand market. They then undertook production of Leslie Hounsfield's Trojan (qv) on a royalty basis until 1928 when they gave notice to Trojan Ltd to vacate the site.

In December 1930 Leyland announced that they were putting a new commercial vehicle into production at Ham, this was the Cub, which was produced throughout the thirties. Six-cylinder petrol engines were initially offered, supplemented in 1934 by a four-cylinder version. In 1931 a six-wheeled model with optional forward-control, refuse vehicles and a tipper were all added to the range as was a fire engine chassis. A diesel engine was offered

186

in 1933 and in 1935 a new light-weight ohv engine using aluminium components was produced. Pantechnicon bodies for house removers and fire engine bodies were built on site up to 1939. In April that year Leyland built the very first airport tender at Ham, for Speke, Liverpool. During WWII munitions and tanks were produced in the factory and in 1946 Leyland and AEC formed a new company, British United Traction, to produce trolleybus chassis at Ham. In January 1948 it was anounced that the facory was to close, production being transferred to the Leyland factory in Lancashire and to AEC at Southall. A London service depot was retained at Ham until 1951. The site had returned to Hawker ownership, the successors to Sopwith, when the lease ran out in 1949. Aircraft production continued until 1991, when the factory was demolished and in 1993 the site was redeveloped.

LISTER: Cambridge (1954–1958), Leatherhead (1983 to date). (See Chapter Eleven).

LMB: LMB Components Ltd. Guildford (1960–1962). Leslie Ballamy had been renowned since the thirties for his improvements to production chassis, particularly conversions of Ford tranverse-leaf spring cars to independent front suspension. He also worked for Allard at Putney. In 1960 he moved into a new factory in Guildford and laid down 100 tubular ladder chassis suitable for either Ford side valve or overhead valve, or BMC 'B' series, engines. Proprietary fibreglass bodies were used. In 1961 an agreement was reached with Edwards Brothers of Tunstall in Staffordshire, whereby cars were assembled with their two/four seat GT body and marketed as the EB Debonair.

LOLA: E. Broadley, Bromley (1958), Lola Cars Ltd. Bromley and Byfleet (1958–1961), Bromley (1961–1965), Slough (1965 to date). In 1958 Eric Broadley built a sports-racing car for the Ford 100E class, winning every race he drove in. In 1959 Coventry Climax-engined versions swept all before them. In 1962 a Formula 1 team was sponsored by Bowmaker, John Surtees putting up some commendable performances. In 1963 the sensational GT Coupé appeared with a Ford V-6 engine behind the driver. In 1966 Graham Hill won the Indy 500 in a Type 90 and in 1967 the Type 100 was introduced. This was a single-seat version of the Type 70, brought out in 1965, and was highly successful in Group 7 sports car events. It was fitted with a

5.5 litre Chevrolet engine which led to a long-running association, continuing today, where Indy cars are built by Lola under a variety of US names.

MACKSON: McGee Refrigeration Ltd. Guildford (1952–1956). The Mackson 500 was a Formula 3 racing car designed by Gordon Bedson with a tubular frame and swing-axle suspension. It was raced by Ken Wharton but successes were few.

MARLBOROUGH THOMAS: T B André & Co. Weybridge (1923–1924). Marlborough had been in existence in London since 1906, selling and later building French designed cars. The shock-absorber firm of André took over the agency in 1909, the firm carrying on until 1926. The Marlborough-Thomas appeared as a separate venture when André and Parry Thomas, operating from a shed at Brooklands, produced a handful of exciting sports-racing cars with 1.5 litre, 4-cylinder, twin ohc engines. The low-built bodies were aerodynamically very efficient and pleasing to the eye. The car was shown at Olympia in 1923, priced at £675.

MARTIN: Hall & Martin, East Croydon (1905–1906). Hall & Martin were car and motorcycle dealers who assembled a small number of cars using 10/12 hp 2-cylinder Aster engines with shaft drive and fitted with four-seat touring bodies.

MASTRA: Trojan Ltd. Croydon (1935). This was an advanced design shown at the 1935 Motor Show which never went into production. It had a 2.2 litre 6-cylinder two-stroke rear-mounted engine and was fitted with a heater and four-wheel jacks, a complete contrast to the very basic Trojan which had then been in production for 12 years.

McLAREN: Trojan Ltd. Croydon (1964–1974), McLaren Cars Ltd. Croydon, (1974–1980), McLaren International Woking (1980–1984), TAG McLaren Group Woking (1984 to date). (See Chapter Eleven).

MOTOR TRACTION Ltd. New Addington (1930–1950). This firm made specialist commercial vehicles to order during the 1930s and 1940s. They were best known for their 'Rutland Clipper', a bus chassis using bought-in parts. There was a choice of Perkins, Meadows, Gardner or AEC engines. Bodies were supplied by Whitson of West Drayton, now under Heathrow Airport. Both businesses failed in 1950.

MURPHY: Nelco Ltd. Guildford Road, Farnham (1936–1980 ?). Len Murphy designed the 'Servitor' electric delivery vehicle, founding Nelco to manufacture it. It was supplied with either a baker's or milkman's body for £125 or £120. The 'Trader' cost £215 for the milk version, or £ 225 for the Baker. In the 1950s Nelco made the 'Solocar', a battery-driven invalid carriage with a range of 35 miles. It sold particularly well in South Africa.

NORDEC: North Downs Engineering Co. Whyteleafe (1949). This company were the sole manufacturers of the Bellamy patented suspension and of Marshall-Nordec superchargers. Both of these components were used in the car which had a Ford 10 engine in a Ford 8 chassis with independent front suspension. The two-seat body looked like a scaled down Allard and was priced at £650. It never went into production.

ONWARD: South Croydon (c 1908). I have only seen one reference to this car which gave no details, giving rise to the thought that perhaps it only existed on paper and was never built.

OSTERFIELD; Douglas S. Cox, West Norwood (1906–1909). Cox moved into the old Weller factory where he built 19.6 hp 4-cylinder and 40 hp 8-cylinder cars, the latter costing £850 just for the chassis. He had previously been involved with the Emerald (qv).

PALLADIUM: Palladium Autocars Ltd. Kensington (1912–1919), Putney (1919–1925). The first cars were assembled from French made components, with 4-cylinder engines of either 10, 12 or 15 hp. A 6-cylinder model was introduced in 1916 and in 1919 an interesting cyclecar powered by a flat-twin air-cooled 1.3 litre engine. In 1922 a conventional 12 hp 4-cylinder Dorman engined light tourer was introduced. It had a 4-speed gearbox, unusual in a light car of the period, and achieved 60 mph with a tuned engine. Fortunately this refinement coincided with the adoption of front wheel brakes, being one of the first British cars to be so fitted.

PANTHER: Panther Westwinds Ltd. Byfleet (1972–1980), Panther Car Co. Byfleet (1980–1990), Korea (1990–   ). Robert Jankel introduced the Panther J72 in 1972 based on the pre-war

Jaguar SS100, with a 3.8 litre 6-cylinder Jaguar engine. In 1974 a 5.3 litre 12-cylinder Jaguar engine was offered as an option. In 1975 the de Ville, a 4-door sports saloon with a Jaguar KJ12 engine, and looks reminiscent of a Type 46 Bugatti, was added to the range. Included in the price of £17,650 was air-conditioning and electric windows. By 1980 the price had reached £67,000. Several other models based on earlier Triumph, Ferrari and Lancia designs were built in very small numbers. In 1977 the astonishing Super Six was introduced. It had six wheels and a mid-mounted 8.2 litre Cadillac engine developing 600 bhp with the assistance of two Garrett turbochargers. The Lima, looking much like a Morgan, but with a fibre glass body, a Vauxhall 2.3 litre slant four engine and MG Midget doors was introduced in 1972, and priced at £4,495 augured well. By 1979 a 178 bhp turbocharged version was also offered, but financial problems loomed and in 1980 Young C Kim's Jindo Industries took over. The more expensive models were dropped and the only type offered was the Kallista, a simplified Lima, now with aluminium body panels supplied from South Korea to Byfleet where the chassis was built. Engines were now either Ford 96 bhp XR3 or 2.3 litre Granada V-6's. The price in 1982 was £5,850 and by 1990 1,672 Limas and Kallistas had been built when the Byfleet production was closed down and transferred to South Korea.

PASSAT: Wimbledon (1910). This was a project to build a car with 'folding wings' which never came to fruition. Perhaps as well that it did not! The mind boggles.

PILGRIM: Pilgrim's Way Motor Co. Ltd. Farnham (1906–1914). The first Pilgrims were large town cars with under-seat engines. The 5.5 litre 4-cylinder unit was mounted horizontally across the frame with the cylinders pointing forward, driving a 2-speed epicyclic pre-selector gearbox. Eighteen cars had been built by 1911 when the company turned to building a 10/12 hp two-seater with front-wheel drive, looking similar to the Renault of the period.

PINZGAUER: Automotive Technik Ltd. (ATL), Guildford (2000–to date). When the Austrian manufacturer Steyr Puch planned, after nearly thirty years in production, to stop making their huge 4 and 6-wheeled all terrain vehicles, the British importers decided to continue building in this country as there was still considerable worldwide demand for the vehicles and for

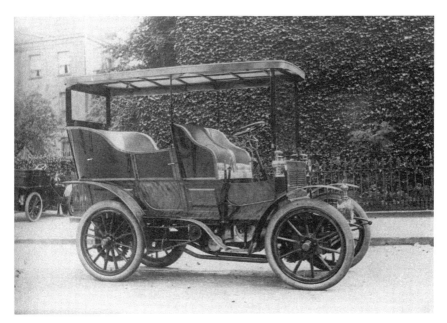

Pilgrim c 1910 *Chris Shepheard collection*

Inside the Pilgrim factory *Chris Shepheard collection*

spares for earlier models. The British army is among the major customers for these rugged machines. Guildford was chosen as it is close to the army test ranges at Chobham, to the MOD in London, and to Heathrow and Gatwick airports. ATL transferred the research, design, assembly and marketing operations for this range to the old Dennis site on the Middleton estate. Bodies for the all terrain vehicles are built by the firm at Fareham, the chassis build and final assembly being undertaken in Guildford. Some 30,000 6x6 and 4x4 vehicles have been built by Steyr Puch since 1971 and are in use worldwide by military and emergency services. The Austrian firm have retained parts manufacture and supply for some European customers.

PROGRESS: Progress Motors Croydon (1930–1934). The Supreme was a 3-seat, 3-wheeled 'economy' car with tiller steering and chain drive. No reverse was fitted. It had previously been built by the same firm in Manchester as the Seal. It was used mainly as a tradesman's delivery vehicle.

RAILTON: Railton Cars Cobham (1933–1939), Hudson Motors London 1940–1949). Railtons were the work of Reid Railton, well-known as designer of World Land Speed Record cars at Brooklands, and were assembled in the old Invicta works at Fairmile, Cobham. The chassis and engine was initially a US Hudson 4 litre Terraplane 8, the body typically British with a rectangular radiator and a row of rivets along the bonnet, reminiscent of the Invicta. The car was capable of 90 mph and

Fairmile Cottage, Cobham, home of Invicta and Railton *Peter Tarplee collection*

Railton 8 Fairmile drop-head coupe 1936, truly a beautiful car *National Motor Museum*

could be driven almost anywhere in top gear. In 1934 the tourer, now fitted with the Hudson 4.2 litre engine, sold for £535. Other Hudson improvements were later incorporated, for example hydraulic brakes in 1936.

The cars grew heavier and more expensive, the saloon in 1936 was now £698. Cheaper versions were introduced in 1938 with the Hudson 2.7 litre 6-cylinder engine and in 1939 the 'baby' Railton was introduced with Standard engine and components. It sold for £299. Post war a handful of Railtons were assembled by Hudson, but restrictions on dollar imports killed it off. It was pre-war the best of the Anglo-American hybrids, some 1,400 cars in total being built. The Metropolitan Police Flying Squad were perhaps the most famous users of the marque.

RAPPORT: Rapport Engineering Ltd. Woking (1980). This company specialised in converting existing models such as Range Rovers into convertibles, much as Abbott had done earlier with Fords. The Ritz was based on a Honda saloon with automatic transmission, air-conditioning, a turbocharged engine, an electrically-operated front spoiler and hydraulically-operated metal top. A GM gearbox was fitted as standard on all models.

ROBINSON & HOLE: Robinson & Hole Ltd. Thames Ditton (1906–1907). Designed by Angus Maitland this car used a 16/20hp T-head 4-cylinder engine and shaft drive. Two and five-seater tourer bodies were offered, but only six cars were completed. A projected 24/30hp model was never built. Maitland then moved to Beacon Hill Motors.

RNW: RNW Products Ltd. Farnham (1951). Designed by R N Wellington this was a two-seat minicar powered by a 197cc Villiers engine at the rear. It had all-round independent suspension, but only two-wheel brakes.

RTC: René Tondeur Co. Ltd. Croydon (1922–1923). This cyclecar was powered by an 8.8 hp air-cooled V-twin Blackburne engine with transmission by direct belt drive to the rear axle. It was claimed that a centrifugal governor automatically varied the effective diameter of the belt pulleys, thus providing a variable gear.

RYNER WILSON: Ryner Wilson Motor Co. Ltd. Wimbledon (1920–1921). This car hardly progressed beyond the prototype stage, but it had a number of unusual features. The engine was a 6-cylinder 15.7 hp 2,290cc unit utilising push-rod operated overhead valves grouped in sets of four on the heads of each pair of cylinders. Two Vici carburetors were used, lubrication was on the dry-sump principle.

SAFIR: Safir Weybridge (1981–1982). This was a road-going version replica of the Ford GT40 road-racing car fitted with a Ford 4.7 litre engine. Very few were sold, priced at £42,500.

SCAMP: Scamp Brookwood (1970–1978). This was an offshoot of Connaught Engineering and manufactured a derivation of the BMC Mini-Moke. It could easily be converted into a 6-wheeler by bolting on a chassis extension. Over 700 were built.

SHADOW: Old Woking and Walton on Thames (early 1920's). An early cyclecar of which no details are available.

SHEEN: In the Woking area (1963). No details are available other than that they produced a 2-seat aluminium-bodied Hillman Imp, probably similar to the Californian produced by Hillman itself a couple of year's later.

SHEFFIELD-SIMPLEX: West Norwood (1907). This was the renamed Brotherhood car and production was removed to Sheffield after only a few of the rebadged models had been produced in Surrey.

SILVER HAWK: Silver Hawk Motors Ltd. Cobham (1920–1921). Noel Macklin set out to build an out-and-out sports car without any pretence of it being a touring car. This was highly unusual and met with its expected fate. The car was basically similar to the Eric-Campbell, which Macklin had been involved with before branching out on his own. The car had a tuned 10/35 hp engine in a dashing aluminium body. Macklin was next to be involved with the Invicta.

SIMPLIC; Wadden & West, Cobham (1914–1915) and Weybridge (1921–1923). True to its name, this was a very simple cyclecar powered by an air-cooled JAP engine. Epicyclic gears were used and the final drive was by a belt. George Wadden had been involved with the Autotrix (qv) in Weybridge before setting up in Cobham on the site of the present Sainsbury petrol station. After the war Wadden returned to Weybridge, this time to Jessamy Road.

SNOW: Baseby and Sadler, Morland Road, Croydon (1920). A light car of which no details are available. It probably did not progress beyond the design stage.

SPEEDY: Pullinger Engineering Co. Ltd. Peckham and Putney (1920–1921). Another cyclecar, announced with a great flourish with plans to build 5,000 in the first year, but only a few were actually made. It had an 8 hp air-cooled V-twin engine, a 2-speed gearbox and belt drive. It was priced competitively at £150.

STACK: G F Stack & Co. East Croydon (1921–1925). This light car had a 766cc V-twin engine and friction transmission, with a device to vary the pressure of the driving disc according to the ratio selected. Final drive was by means of a single chain.

STAINES-SIMPLEX: Staines Motor Co. Staines (1906–1908). Two models were built, but production was erratic. An article in *The Motor* at the time suggested that the company was more interested in hiring out machines and that production only occurred when the chauffeurs employed by the company were otherwise idle.

STYLUS: Specialist Sports Cars Ltd. Guildford (1996). A sports car in the Surrey tradition based on a space-frame chassis. It won five race championships in as many years. The car had modern suspension giving excellent traction and fine acceleration with a good weight balance between engine and gearbox. It weighed only 640 kgs and has been described as "blisteringly fast and surefooted, an ideal road and competition car". Many different engine choices were offered and the car was available as a kit for around £6,000 or could be built to order.

SURREY: West London Scientific Apparatus Co. Ltd Putney (1921–1922), Surrey Service Ltd. Putney (1922–1927), Surrey Light Cars, Putney (1927–1930). The Surrey was an assembled car using Ford Model T parts, and powered by a 4-cylinder Coventry-Simplex engine. Electric lighting and starting were optional extras as late as 1923, by which time friction drive had been replaced by a Meadows gearbox and a live axle. Later cars had V-radiators and Meadows engines of 9.8 and 11.8 hp.

SWEETZER-BAKER: Reigate (1908). I can find no written reference to this garage firm ever building a car, merely a verbal one, but from a reputable source.

TAMPLIN: Tamplin Motors Ltd. Staines (1912–1923), Cheam (1923–1927). This cyclecar was a direct descendant of the pre-war Carden. It was at first a tandem two-seater with a centrally-mounted 980cc V-twin JAP engine, with chain primary and belt final drive. In 1922 it became a more orthodox vehicle with side-by-side seating, all-chain drive and front-mounted engine. A sports version in 1923 had a polished aluminium body and a Blackburne engine. Some 2,000 cars were built and was said to still be available after 1927 to special order.

TIGER: Cartel Group Woking (1983). The Turbo Intercooled Ground Effect car was a two-seat sports car looking like a Grand Prix car and fitted with a Renault 2.7 litre V-6 engine with twin turbochargers and intercooling giving some 235 bhp. It was designed by Chris Humberstone, who was also responsible for the design of the 'Popemobiles'.

THURLOW: Thurlow & Co. Wimbledon (1914–1921). A prototype 3-wheeler appeared in 1914 but production did not start until after the war. It had a 10hp V-twin Precision engine driving a 3-speed Sturmey-Archer gearbox. Final drive was by belts.

TOURETTE: Carr Bros. Purley (1956). Progress Supreme Co. Ltd. Purley (1957-1958). A very light three-wheeler with a 197cc Villiers engine and 4-speed gearbox and optional reverse. Bodies were either plastic or aluminium on an ash frame, priced at £299 or £325. The cheaper model was the least expensive car then available in Britain, but it did not sell, customers preferring something more substantial if more expensive.

TROJAN: Leyland Motors Ltd. Kingston (1922–1928), Trojan Ltd. Croydon (1928–1965). The Trojan, designed by Leslie Hounsfield, was a rare case of an extremely unconventional design selling well and holding a good-sized and faithful market for some years. The Leyland Company, well known for both its heavy commercial lorries and the ultra-luxurious Eight car, had taken over the redundant National Aircraft Factory in Richmond Road, Kingston, to rebuild over 3,000 of their 'G' type vehicles supplied to the military during WWI. There was no spare capacity at the Leyland works in Lancashire, hence the move to Kingston.

There was spare capacity at Kingston and Hounsfield

Trojan advertising van c 1924 – note the solid tyres, almost unique by this time *Tim Harding*

Trojan detachable hardtop c 1926 *Tim Harding*

negotiated for the building there of his Trojan Utility car, of which he had built three models only in Croydon in 1913. He joined Leyland as Chief Engineer and assisted them in moving to the other end of the car market. The Trojan was aimed at simplicity in driving and maintenance at a low price. The horizontal 2-stroke, 4-cylinder, engine was mounted under the floor. It had a cubic capacity of 1.5 litres but only developed 110 bhp. Transmission was by a 2-speed epicyclic gearbox and double chains to a solid axle. Although the engine was slow-reving, such power as it developed came in at very low engine speeds. Its low-speed pulling power and hill-climbing ability became legendary.

Its oddities went much further. For the sake of cheapness solid tyres were fitted up to 1929, pneumatic tyres being an optional extra up to then. The chassis was a flat steel box to which was attached a roomy, if hideous, open four-seat body. By 1925 the price was still only £125, making it the cheapest British four-seater on the market. It was also the slowest and never had front wheel brakes, but its advantages outweighed its drawbacks for many customers who cared nothing for appearance.

In 1928, when production was up to 100 cars a week, manufacture was transferred to Croydon. By the thirties the market was hardening for unconventional cars so a more modern, conventional, design was produced. This was the RE 'Purley' saloon, which retained the old engine and transmission but fitted with a good-looking fabric body, the engine was rear-

Post WWII Trojan van *Chris Shepheard collection*

mounted driving forward by chain. There were three forward gears, balloon tyres and half-eliptic springs. It still lacked four-wheel brakes and was more expensive. It did not succeed in the market place even when a centrifugal clutch was fitted in 1932 and a fluid flywheel two years later.

At the 1935 Motor Show the car was replaced by the Mastra, a 2.2litre 6-cylinder car. It was still rear-engined but had synchromesh gears, a heater and built-in jacks. It never went into production and no more passenger cars were built until 1962 when the Heinkel 'bubble' car was built under the Trojan name and the Elva (qv) sports car was produced, both until 1965 when the association with McLaren (qv) started.

Trojan produced a range of vans on the Utility chassis, most having distinctive bodies, that for Bass in the shape of a beer bottle and for Brook Bond Tea painted in garish colours. A modern van was produced in the 1960s but did not find much favour.

TYRRELL: Ockham (1959-1998). (See Chapter Eleven).

UTILE: Utile Motor Manufacturing Co. Ltd. Kew Gardens (1904). This light car had an 8 hp single-cylinder engine of the de Dion type. It had two speeds but one was said to be enough for 'normal' running. Final drive was by shaft and a two-seat body was fitted.

VICTORIA: Victoria Motor Works, Godalming (1907). This was an assembled car with a 10/12 hp 4-cylinder Fafnir engine with overhead inlet valves and shaft drive. Fitted with a tourer body it sold for £300.

WARREN LAMBERT: Warren Lambert Engineering Co. Ltd. Shepherds Bush (1912–1914), Richmond (1919–1922). This car started life as a typical cyclecar with a water-cooled Blumfield 2-cylinder engine and shaft drive. By 1914 a Dorman 4-cylinder engine was fitted and production was 25 per week. After the war the firm restarted in Richmond using an Alpha 4-cylinder 1,330 cc engine and then produced a striking super sports car with a 1.5 litre Coventry Simplex engine with an enormous burnished copper exhaust pipe. Supply difficulties forced the car out of production in 1922.

WELLER: Weller Brothers, West Norwood (1903). The company made motor cycles and one model of car, with a 20 hp 4-cylinder engine and double chain drive. The engine and gearbox was fitted on an underframe separate from the chassis. Although 8, 10 and 15 hp models were advertised, only the 20 hp version was actually built. John Weller subsequently went on to found Autocarriers in North London, the forerunner of AC Cars of Thames Ditton (qv).

WHITEHEAD THANET: Amalgamated Motors Ltd. Ashtead (1920–1921). This was one of the most ambitious of the post-war schemes to manufacture mass-produced cars, but there is no firm evidence that even one car was built. The company was set up by A J Whitehead, who had made a fortune during the war making aircraft parts and assemblies, with ambitious plans to make 5,000 cars a month by 1920, rising to 100,000 a year by the end of 1921. Parts not otherwise bought in were to be made at Richmond, with assembly at Ashtead. The car was to have an American chassis from the Gray Andrews Corporation and an English 16/20hp 4-cylinder engine with coachwork by F J Wraight of London. Wraights are listed in some reference books as the makers of the Thanet car. Unfortunately the grand plan never got off the drawing board.

WHITGIFT: Croydon Central Motor Co. Ltd., Croydon (1913). This was a low-built cyclecar with an 8 hp V-twin JAP engine, friction transmission and chain drive to the offside rear wheel.

WILBURY: Redhill (1900). An early kit car with a 5hp engine which could be assembled by cycle dealers.

WINGFIELD: Wingfield Motor Co. Norbury (1909–1912), Cars & Motor Sundries Ltd. (1912–1920). The first model with an 18/23hp 4-cylinder engine appeared in 1909 but did not go immediately into production. In 1912 the business changed hands and the new owners planned to build 250 cars a year. By 1914 four 4-cylinder and three 6-cylinder models were advertised, but it is uncertain how many, if any, were actually made. In 1920 a prototype 23.8 hp six was built but nothing more was heard of it, or of the company.

XTRA: Xtra Cars Ltd. Chertsey (1922–1924). This simple cyclecar was no more than a single-seat side car mounted on a three-wheeled chassis. The 3.5 hp Villiers engine and 2-speed transmission were mounted on the rear wheel.

ZENDIK: Zendik Cars Ltd. Kingston (1913–1914). Another cyclecar with an 8 hp Chater-Lea 2-cylinder engine and a two speed transmission with direct drive in top, and chain reduction for bottom, whilst reverse was by engaging overhead worm gearing on the rear axle.

ZENITH: Zenith Cars Ltd. Kingston (1905–1906). This company made motor cycles and a two-seat car with a 6 hp 2-cylinder Stevens engine.

The Humbee Surrey, in spite of its name was not made in the county or even in Britain. It was a three-wheeled light car, also built as a van, by the Mitsui Seike Kogyo Co. Ltd., Tokyo, Japan between 1950 and 1962.

One possible entry is the **ARAB (1926–1928).** Georgano states that this potent sports car, with a 1,960cc 4-cylinder engine designed by Reid Railton, was built in small numbers, probably no more than 12, in Letchworth, Hertfordshire. It had an electric fuel pump, which was rare for the period. However a letter from Kenneth McGuffie in the February 1959 issue of *Motor Sport* refers to an Arab, bodied and owned by his brother

Chota McGuffie, which had a chassis by Thompson and Taylor of Brooklands. (*The correct spelling should be Thomson*).

According to the letter Chota McGuffie had a firm in Wimbledon in the twenties, called either A P Compton & Co. Ltd. or Arrow Coachworks Ltd., and built bodies on two Arab chassis which had come from Brooklands, having lain there for a year or more. McGuffie says that the car had an amazing acceleration and a top speed of 94 mph. The car owned by his brother had become a total loss after hitting a lamp-standard near Buckingham Palace. It appears that the Arab could qualify as a Surrey car if, as it seems, that probably all the chassis were built at Brooklands, there is no record of where the Railton-designed engines were built, and ten or more were assembled in Letchworth and two in Wimbledon. R H Beauchamp, in '25 Years at Brooklands Track', states "It was not long after the formation of Thomson & Taylor (Brooklands) Ltd. that the position of Chief Designer was filled by Mr. Reid A Railton ... who was beginning to produce the Arab car in small numbers at Letchworth". This would have been in 1927 and adds to the complex story of the Arab.

Also worth a mention, though not strictly a car manufacturer, was W Galloway & Co. Ltd, in Ashtead from 1912 to 1916. Galloway, a Tyneside bolt and screw manufacturer, obtained a licence to import kits of US Stanley steam cars and build them for sale in this country. A London showroom was set up and a repair and overhaul workshop in Ashtead, as most customers were in the south of the country. War conditions from 1914 made supplies from the US erratic and the business closed in 1916. Surplus boilers in stock were adapted to drive pumps in the trenches on the western front. 1918 saw the end of steam cars.

Appendix II

Component Manufacturers

Behind every good man there is said to be a good woman and behind every front-line soldier there are at least ten support staff. So with car building, behind each manufacturer there are numerous component makers. Surrey has had a share of these, some of the more significant are listed below, in no particular order of size or date.

KLG. Kenelm Lee Guiness set up his own factory in Roehampton Vale on the site of The Bald Faced Stag inn, in the nineteen twenties, to manufacture spark plugs and other electrical equipment for his own racing cars. Existing plugs with porcelain insulation would not stand up to the high temperatures in racing engines so Guiness' brother Bill developed a plug using thin layers of mica for insulation. In time the lead which was subsequently introduced into petrol led to a breakdown of the mica so new porcelain insulation was developed, which saved the day. The factory was subsequently bought out by Smiths Industries and was closed in the nineteen eighties. The site has been redeveloped as an ASDA store and for Kingston University.

BLACKBURNE. The Burney brothers, backed by Harold Blackburn – a noted pioneer aviator – set up Burney and Blackburn in 1912 to manufacture a motorcycle in Berkhampstead from a design by Geoffrey de Havilland. Blackburn moved on to work with another Blackburn, Robert who was no relation, to set up an aircraft manufacturing business in Brough, Yorkshire. In 1913 the Burneys moved to Tongham when the name of the firm was changed to Burney and Blackburne, with an 'e' to avoid confusion. Meanwhile Tom Gillett had set up an engineering business at the Atlas Works, Little Bookham, becoming a limited company, Gillett Stephen & Co., in 1912. During WWI more space was needed for the manufacture of aircraft engine and other parts so the former Merrylands Hotel, opposite Bookham station and now part of the modern Industrial Estate, was acquired, becoming the New Atlas Works.

In 1919 production of the Blackburne motor cycle was transferred to the Osborn Engineering Co. of Gosport who marketed it first under the Blackburne name and then as the OEC. Production of Blackburne engines for motor cycles, cars, aircraft and agricultural machines was taken over by Gillett Stephens in Bookham. Blackburne engines were used by over sixty different motor cycle manufacturers and a number of

Inside the Thomson & Taylor workshops at Brooklands c1937 *Chris Shepheard collection*

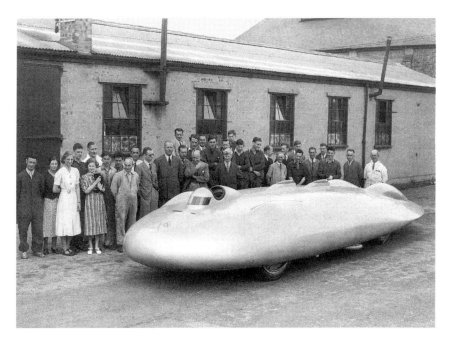

The Railton Mobil Special with Thomson & Taylor staff 1938 *Brooklands Museum*

cyclecar builders. They also built 4-cylinder engines for ABC cars and 6-cylinder ones for Invicta and Frazer Nash as well as for some twenty odd other car firms. In the twenties they also reconditioned WWI Liberty aero engines for use in racing cars and naval torpedo boats. Dennis and Merryweather used Blackburne engines for fire appliances and trailer pumps.

Aircraft parts were being made again during the thirties and by 1936 demand for these was so high that production of Blackburne engines was stopped, never to re-start. The factory made aircraft parts during WWII and after was occupied by a number of different engineering firms until in 1989 the site was taken over by Photo-Me International and is today their worldwide repair and maintenance base. During the thirties **GOODHEW & SONS** also operated from the Atlas Works where they undertook motor body repairs.

THOMSON & TAYLOR (Brooklands) Ltd. Ken Thomson was a friend of J G Parry Thomas and worked with him on the Leyland Thomas, the Thomas Specials and 'Babs', helping to set up the Thomas Inventions Development Co. (Chapter Seven qv). Thomson & Taylor Ltd. was established in 1927 with Reid

Railton as Chief Designer and is best remembered for its work with Campbell and Cobb constructing their land speed record-breaking cars in the 1930s. (Chapter Eight qv). The name continued in a garage business in Cobham from after the war until the end of the century, latterly as a BMW franchise. The business continues today under new owners.

WEYBURN BARTEL. Down a leafy lane near Elstead, west of Guildford, and at Eashing, near Godalming, this firm was started during WWI to make connecting rods, and continued to do so as part of Carborundum Ltd, the third largest maker of con rods in the world.

PULLMAN. Based in the Westbrook leather mill, Godalming, the site of the first town public electricity supply in 1886, the firm moved into rubber 'non-skid covers' or 'bands'. Roads were atrocious in the early days of motoring and the bands were advertised to be fastened over the covers by means of straps held taut by chains. An advertisement claimed 'as fitted to a car of His Majesty The King. The band can be fitted to your car in four days or supplied complete with outer cover from stock.' Pullmans remained in business until after WWII having made flexible fuel drop-tanks for aircraft during the war.

DRUMMOND. This Guildford firm, set up in 1882, was famous for its lathes. Many of its four inch models were bought by early motorists to make parts for their cars. Generally it was the chauffeur who turned his hand to repairs of his master's car.

WALKER. James Walker of Woking made seals, gaskets and packing for the motor and other industries until recently on an historic site when it was redeveloped and they moved elsewhere. It was first the Oriental Institute of Dr. Gottlieb Leitner, in 1910 was taken over by the Accumulator Supply Co. and then by Martin and Handyside, the WWI aircraft manufacturers. Walkers moved in during the nineteen twenties.

VOKES. This maker of filters was bombed out of London during WWII and set up at Lord Henley's empty house at Broad Street near Guildford. Here they continued to make air and oil filters for aircraft and road vehicles. New buildings were erected in 1958 and the product range expanded. The firm was taken over by the Thomas Tilling Group, themselves subsequently by the

BTR Group in 1983. Today's production is for non-vehicular use, air conditioning plants, marine diesel engines and nuclear power plants.

TDC COMPONENTS Ltd. Bill Terry set up a racing car body-building business in Kingston after WWI with Harry Hawker. After WWII he joined Vic Derrington to make exhaust systems and to tune race cars. The firm made exhausts for Connaught, Cooper and Lotus.

BOURDON. This Bramley firm made gauges of all types for the motor and general engineering industries.

J L JAMESON. This firm was in Ewell and Chessington from the 1930s to the 1960s and made small flat four aero engines of their own design during WWII, and later undercarriage components for Vickers Aircraft. They are reputed to have made parts for Campbell's Bluebirds during the 'thirties.

JACK KNIGHT DEVELOPMENTS. A Woking firm started in 1946 which made parts for the first Jordan racing car.

GOMM METAL DEVELOPMENTS Ltd. of Old Woking have been in motor racing for some fifty years, during which time they have turned out metal work for everything from racing cars to submarines.

BRIFEX Ltd. This Ashtead firm made leathercloth for bus and car seats from 1926 to 1972, when they closed and the buildings were converted into offices.

SYKES GEARS. This firm started in Egham making gears initially for Lagonda, moving later to larger premises in Staines where it made a wide range of gears for the motor and general engineering industries. Both sites are now redeveloped.

There are currently three businesses on the Bookham Industrial Estate with motoring interests. **ASHLEY-HINTON PANELS** bought up the tooling when the MG factory in Abingdon closed some years ago. They now supply a large and continuing market for replacement panels for MG B and Midget cars. **BARWELL MOTORSPORT** are involved in several different aspects of motorsport. They have been in existence for over 30 years, moving to Bookham in 1999, and now run a successful Formula BMW team with the assistance of Tiff Needell. The firm also prepares and maintains race, rally and road cars, offers specialist fabrication and machining services, car rebuilds and restoration and employs a professional test driver for circuit tuition, chassis evaluation and set up. In addition they are the official European Fitting Centre for Spoon Sports Honda performance parts. The Barwell BTCC team uses Spoon Sports products on its race-winning Honda Civic Type R racing cars.

DPS COMPOSITES is a high-tech business and one of the largest independent motorsport composite manufacturers in the world. They design, engineer and produce a wide range of carbon fibre components for many of the world's leading manufacturers. The firm was founded in 1987 by David Price and Phil Sharp, the latter then working for McLaren where John Barnard had designed the world's first carbon fibre chassis, the MP4. DPS produced the body panels for the McLaren F1 road car and in 2003 produced all the tooling for the new MG X80 Power SV sports car. Some panels are being produced in Italy, where the chassis is being assembled, others in Britain, where the final assembly takes place. DPS also work for Ford and Yamaha and manufacture the Voodoo Military Target Drone, housing for a Naval Radar System, an Aerotech Wind Tunnel Arm, the Lotus Track Bike and medical products.

In 1987 the **FERRARI DESIGN CENTRE** was established at Shalford when John Barnard, who had moved from McLaren on being appointed Chief Designer, refused to work permanently in Italy. When he did not renew his contract the Centre was moved to Modena in Italy, the home of Ferrari. Barnard then set up the **BENETTON DESIGN CENTRE** which was until recently based in Godalming, but it too moved when taken over by Renault, in this case to Oxford to be nearer the manufacturing site.

ROYAL ARMY RESEARCH & DEVELOPMENT ESTABLISHMENT. Western Surrey has been military territory for many years and the Chobham site of MVEE (Military Vehicle Experimental Establishment), owned by the Ministry of Defence, is where tank trials are carried out and where 'Chobham Armour' was developed.

References

Again my sources have been many and varied, written and verbal, including that modern marvel – the Internet. Francis Haveron had identified several businesses in and around Godalming and Guildford, whilst Peter Tarplee's article 'The Atlas Works, Bookham and Blackburne Engines' in the 2002 Proceedings of the Leatherhead & District Local History Society, Vol.6, No. 6, provided much information on Blackburne, adding to that I already had. '25 Years at Brooklands Track' by R H Beauchamp, was helpful with information on Thomson & Taylor (Brooklands) Ltd.

Acknowledgements

My thanks to all those who willingly provided illustrations –
Brooklands Museum, The National Motor Museum, Chertsey
Museum, Egham Museum, The Museum of Farnham, Roger
Heard and Transbus Dennis and Tim Harding of Croydon. To
John Pulford at Brooklands and Jonathan Day at the National
Motor Museum for their help in selecting suitable prints. To Pam
Haveron for enabling me to undertake the book by so willingly
passing over Francis Haveron's notes and research papers. My
thanks particularly to Chris Shepheard and Peter Tarplee of
SIHG for supplying illustrations and for their careful reading of
the text and their helpful and useful comments on some of the
facts and style.

Index

Homfray-Davis, R A 166
Honda 142, 152, 153, 154, 193, 208
Hong Kong 98, 104, 106
Honolulu 98
Hooper 164
Hopkirk, Paddy 135
Horley 23, 181, 185
Horley Motor Co 181
Hornstead 58
Horseless Carriage Company 94
Horsham 13, 25, 32
Hot-Tube Ignition 38, 39, 44
Hounsfield, Leslie 186, 197
Hove 85
Howard Motor Works 181
Howard, Lord 40
Howards of Bedford 37
Howell, C H 9
Howell, Frank 14
Howey, Capt J E P 70, 71
HP see Hilton-Pearcy
HRG 65, 131, 132, 136, 160, 181
Hudson Motors 192, 193
Hulme, Denny 147, 148, 151
Humbee Surrey 201
Humberstone, Chris 196
Humming Bird 181
Humphrey & Tenant 36
Hunt, James 151
Hurlock brothers 115, 120, 123, 124, 125, 128
Hurlock, Charles F 115, 116
Hurlock, Derek 125, 127
Hurlock, W A E 115, 125, 128
Hutton, J E 54, 182
HWM 130, 138, 139, 181
Hyde Park 44, 48

Imperial 182
Indianapolis 55, 83, 147, 165
International Association of Recognised Automobile Clubs 73
Invicta 79, 182, 184, 192, 195, 205
'Iodine Walker' 68
Iso Rivolta 139
Isotta-Fraschini 61
Isotta-Maybach 61
Itala 54, 58, 76, 169, 184
Izod, E G 166

JAG 184
Jaguar 124, 133, 139, 141, 155, 156, 157, 163, 190
Jameson, J L 207
Jamieson, Murray 80, 82
Jankel, Robert 189

Jansson, Jan-Erik 128
JAP 62, 63, 85, 133, 172, 175, 179, 181, 184, 195, 196, 201
Jappic 63, 184
Jarrott, Charles 49
JBM 185
Jekyll, Gertrude 6
Jenatzy 57
Jindo Industries 190
Johannson, Stefan 152
John Dennis Coachbuilders 107
Johnston Sweepers 185
Jones, Col H (VC) 138
Jones, Parnelli 159
Jordan 150, 207
Joyce, J A 113
Judd 149, 150
Junior Car Club 59, 79

Kai Tak Motor Bus Co 104
Kenley 18
Kennet, P 129
Kensington 189
Kent 11, 16, 32, 43, 72, 130, 142, 145, 175
Kent, Ford engine 144
Kerr, Phil 151
Kew 4, 173, 175, 177, 178, 199
'Kim' 59
Kim, Young C 190
Kinch, Nathan 158
King & Taylor 168
King, Baron of Ockham 51
Kingston 5, 7, 10, 11, 13, 15, 16, 17, 18, 23, 24, 25, 26, 30, 35, 65, 113, 130, 131, 171, 173, 180, 186, 187, 197, 201, 203, 207
KLG 203
'KN' 57
Knight, Jack 207
Knight, John Henry 11, 36, 37, 38, 39, 40, 41, 42, 43, 45, 46, 47, 48, 49, 185
Knollys, Lord 47
Kowloon Motor Bus Co 104

La Salle 161
LAD 185
Lagonda 132, 139, 162, 185, 186, 207
Lake, John 93
Lambert, Harold 58
Lambeth 9
Lamborgini 155
Lammas-Graham 85
Lanchester, Frederick 43, 46, 62
Lanchester, George 62